90/-

8 1-7151-151-1

THE URGENCY OF IJTIHAD

Al-Haj Moinuddin Ahmed,
I.A.S. (Retd.)

Produced under the auspices of
The Urdu Education Foundation,
Mission Road, Cuttack-753 001
India

KITAB BHAVAN
NEW DELHI-110 002 (INDIA)

KITAB BHAVAN
Exporters & Importers
1784, Kalan Mahal, Daryaganj
New Delhi-110002 [India]

Phones : 3274686, 3263383
Telex : 31-63106 ALI IN

ISBN 81-7151-151-1

First Published in India 1992

Published by:
Nusrat Ali Nasri for Kitab Bhavan
1784, Kalan Mahal, Daryaganj
New Delhi-110002 [India]

Printed in India at:
Nazia Printers
Rodgran, Lal Kuan
Delhi-110006

إِنَّ اللّٰهَ لَا يُغَيِّرُ مَا بِقَوْمٍ
حَتّٰى يُغَيِّرُوْا مَا بِاَنْفُسِهِمْ ط

"Verily, Allah changeth not the condition of a people until they (first) change their conditions by themselves."

* Holy Qur'an-13 11 *

CONTENTS

FOREWORD

The Worldwide Brotherhood of Islamic Peoples may rightly claim the honour and pride of eminence on two glorious facts about their Religion. The first one is that "The Qur'an is the most widely read book in existence", as observed by European Classical Scholars on Islam like Phillip K. Hitti, Charles Potter and others, none of whom are known for their sympathetic approach to Islam. The second one is that the well-known American Author Prof. Michael H. Hart undertook a serious and extensive study of great men of all times and of all countries ever born in the World. He took note of the features of greatness and distinction of each of them, drew up a list of 100 top-most persons from amongst them, arranged the selected men in order of maximum contribution by them to the advancement of World Civilization, and published the final result in his book "The Hundred". This merit list is headed by Prophet Hazrat Muhammad, being No. 1 among all the men ever born to breathe on the face of the Earth.

Such is the Prophet of Islam, who in the best of his sagacity, made a wise provision in order to maintain the freshness and compatibility of Islamic Laws for all times and all climes. This unique provision based on Qur'anic rudiments, was styled IJTIHAD. It was implemented by the holy Prophet himself, and by Companions, great Imams and divines for 300 years after the lifetime of the Prophet.

About the 4th Century Hijri, some frustrated and motivated Ulama of no good repute, guided by personal considerations, are reported to have convened an assemblage of Ummah and passed a Decree banning the provision of Ijtihad for all time thereafter. The result was that all thinking fresh and looking forward were forbidden and declared sinful. People could look back to the past for seeking guidance for all their present and future needs, but could not advocate, preach or practice any new concept or fresh thought, which were condemned as unholy innovation. The action thus taken is known as "Closing the Gate of Ijtihad".

The saner elements did not agree and raised voice of protest from time to time. Dr Sir Muhammad Iqbal described the move as "Pure Fiction". The present Review, after sustained examination of all aspects, came to the conclusion that the closure of Ijtihad was a measure lacking in Scriptural validity, and was in fact, a hoax played by a band of frustrated Ulama of no good repute. The Review calls for ignoring the so-called 'Decree' and for re-opening the process of Ijtihad in right earnest.

Contents of this book cover some special topics such as God's attributes, Islamic Laws etc. Section III relates to Changeful Universe, particularly for information of obscurantists who believe that since Ijtihad has once been closed by the consensus of Ijma, it can never be re-opened at any time. In fact, this is a mis-conceived idea. God alone is not subject to any change, but every thing else in the Universe, including even the texts of sacred Scriptures and the imperative Commandments of God have undergone change under exceptional circumstances, as shown in Section III. So the decision to close the Gate of Ijtihad can also change if there are good reasons for it. Inclusion of such special topics in the book may prove useful to general readers and particularly to Ijtihad Scholars, who require a broad out- look and clear vision to enable them to formulate new Rulings or to re-interpret old ones correctly, without feeling handicapped for lack of knowledge on allied matters. Moreover, in addition to comprehensive treatment of the principles and operation of Ijtihad, the book copiously deals with knowledgeable matters on the tenets and practice of Islam, so that the reader may become well-informed about the Religion of Islam.

It is the earnest hope of the author that this short book may be perused with patience, and with open and unprejudiced mind. It may perhaps help to free the reader's mind from the clutches of Medievalism, the heritage of confusion and the legacy of long-standing misconceptions if any. He may then draw his own conclusion, and possibly get ready to work for undoing the stagnation that has bedevilled the Islamic Society for over a thousand years.

January, 1992.
Urdu Education Foundation,
Mission Road, Cuttack-753001 Moinuddin Ahmed.

Section I

INTRODUCTORY

Enlightened Muslims feel deeply concerned at the widespread stagnation prevailing in their community-life for Centuries. The malady is prolonged, extensive and persistent, having grasped all spheres of their activities--Religious, social, educational and economic. God-fearing intellectuals and patriots like Allama Shibli Nu'mani, Syed Sulaiman Nadwi, Altaf Hussain Hali, Syed Ameer Ali, Dr Sir Muhammad Iqbal, Sir Syed Ahmad Khan and others died crying for awakening their sleepy community to rise again and resume leadership of the World-stage, where they once stood as the 'Torch-bearers of Civilization'. Eminent Spiritual Leaders and Defenders of Islam like Mujaddid-e-Azam Imam Ghazali, Maulana Jalaluddin Rumi, Shaikh-ul Islam Hafiz Ibn Taimiyah and Shah Waliullah Mohaddis Dehlavi bewailed at the retrogression in Religious practice from the ideals of pristine Islamic Faith held by the Sahaba and the first generation of Believers.

Imam Ghazali held the view that debasement had crept into the study of Theology as the Ulama of his Age had developed sectarian outlook, and were consequently guiding the course of religious education along wrong lines. This view was expressed about a thousand years back when the position was already bad. The continuation of religious education on the same wrong lines ever since then has made matters much worse by now. As a result of mis-leading education all these Centuries, Muslims have been losing ground in the field of Spiritual attainment as well as in worldly achievements, and failing to vie with other communities in different walks of life.

In consequence, the Muslims are left far behind other World communities. Their high illiteracy, growing poverty and habitual conservative mentality to look backwards to days gone by in all eventualities has involved them in a thousand fetters of their own making. Their all-round unprogressive condition has seized them like tentacles of an Octopus, from which retrieval is an unsurmountable task for leaders of the community.

The Holy Qur'an teaches that life is a process of progressive development. Life is not static; it is moving. Movement is a sign of life, a mark of progress, an order of Nature, while denial of movement is an indication of stagnation, a symbol of death. Muslims must not remain stagnant at the level of Medieval Age consciousness. The world has gone far ahead and is confronted today with new forces implanting profound changes in human affairs. The Muslim community must now look forward, re-fashion its general outlook, re-structure its social frame and move out in search of new terms of equality with other World communities. It requires a break-through in perception, a change in intellectual approach in which healthy thinking may thrive. Honestly, the Muslims should not build castles in the air by imagining that they are not concerned with lowly mundane affairs because their centre of attention is the other World. They must not forget that their holy Prophet had achieved ideal success in Worldly life in addition to instilling Religious and Spiritual acumen among a vast section of humanity sunk in the depths of ignorance and profligacy.

It was through emulation of the Prophet's eminent example that Islam could develop within a short span of time from a small Arabian nomadic community to a progressive, prosperous and civilised World Power, simultaneously projecting a major Religious Movement in the World. The basis of such phenomenal advancement in temporal as well as spiritual realm, was the invaluable guidance received from the Holy Qur'an and the holy Prophet, both offering incentive and direction to the Believers to rely on free personal Judgment, next to acting on Scriptural principles.

Exercise of free Judgment is sanctioned by the Holy Qur'an, but is related to certain circumstances only. We have been correctly taught that in all matters relating to Spiritual, Religious and Social conduct, we have first to seek guidance from the injunctions of the Holy Qur'an and thereafter, the precepts of Hadith Literature. This is imperative and there is no question of relying upon one's own Judgment in such matters. The question then arises, how to behave in matters where there is no specific guidance available in sacred Scriptures, the Qur'an and Hadith. The answer has been directly and unambiguously given by the holy Prophet himself, who formulated the relevant legal principle in his life-time. This principle, known as IJTIHAD, worked smoothly for about 300 years. Thereafter, some controversy arose about its limitation by rulings of some later Jurists. The problem, as it now poses, is whether the principle of Ijtihad holds good in the present day as in the days of the holy Prophet, or has been barred by limitation on the basis of a consensus of Jurists of the Medieval Age.

The controversy over termination or continuation of Ijtihad still continues, while the complexities of modern life need clear-cut Judgment on ever-increasing new issues which the old mind is afraid to tackle. The present day Culture as tempered by the latest gifts of Science and Technology, has precipitated new issues, all of which do not find mention in the sacred Scriptures or can not fit squarely into the frame of old Islamic ways of life based on social factors prevailing 1,400 years ago. The old yard-stick of human thought and action now requires re-calibration and re-adjustment in the light of modern trends in intellectual and cultural temperament, which have drastically out-moded many of the old guidelines. An appropriate machinery is needed for restoring relevance to such guidelines. The purpose will be served by bringing into play the process of Ijtihad, so that appropriate interpretations are made whenever old Rulings of conduct appear irrelevant, or new provisions are adopted wherever links are found missing.

Ijtihad thus becomes indispensable, as it will speak where there is silence, and will re-interpret where there is mis-construction, thereby protecting old rulings from being side-tracked and forgotten, and restoring them a value of compatibility with modern trends. The Holy Qur'an permits the Ummah to take dicisions on problems not specifically covered by the Qur'an and Hadith, by adoption of the principle of Ijtihad. But some Jurists of Medieval times under dubious circumstances chose to declare a ban on this Divine provision. As a result, progressive thinking stopped and the dead weight of Medieval attitude kept on piling over the community's socio-religious behavior and outlook from century to century during the past millennium.

Ijtihad was indispensable during the holy Prophet's time. It is all the more so during the present time, when life has become more complex and problematic, and the Muslims feel confused, bewildered and dispirited in all walks of life. Its operation will ensure a harmonious blend of Islamic ideals with present-day requirements, most imperatively needed for the Muslim community afflicted with manifold ailment for many Centuries in the past.

Out of a multitude of problems demanding attention, this small Publication concerns itself with only one particular aspect, namely, the measures necessary for reversing the trend of decline in Muslim society and polity. At the outset, it becomes necessary to identify the factors responsible for such decline. The most important single factor the present study has discovered is the tendency of a vast section of Muslims to imitate old norms blindly, rather than to initiate, formulate or welcome new lines of action promising greater advantage and convenience. They have degenerated to the level of ancestor-imitation, by which every novelty is looked down with contempt and derision. They do not understand that human society can remain useful, vibrant and lively only by reconstructing and adding to its existence, for otherwise it will reach old age and spend its life-capital, till it becomes meaningless as a dead body. Here lies the relevance of Ijtihad in today's life. It helps to renew, invigorate and enliven the human society by contributing elements of freshness and compatibility to the Rules of the society.

In the pages that follow, a dispassionate review has been made of the primary objective of the concept of Ijtihad, and when and how it originated. The historical, theological and rational implications of the Doctrine, the views of orthodox section of Scholars as well as of God-fearing enlightened Intellectuals have also been mentioned. Careful study of the contents is expected to be rewarding for Scholars and general readers alike.

Muslims are already left behind. While the World is dashing ahead in leaps and bounds towards great heights of prosperity of the 21st Century, the Muslims have chained themselves to out-moded concepts of the Medieval past. They should in all seriousness free themselves from fetters of their own making and attune themselves to the modern World trends by adopting the operation of Ijtihad even now, if they want to co-exist with other advanced nations of the World as equal, respectable Citizens.

Section II

GOD'S UNIVERSAL BENEVOLENCE

The Supreme Purpose:

The Universe is the singular inimitable handicraft of the Consummate Artist, God. God's supreme purpose in creation of the Universe is the evolution of the divinely conceived Man as the end product. It was God's utmost pleasure to create Man in the likeness of Himself. Man is the Crown of all the creations. The Holy Qur'an most appropriately acknowledges Man as *'Ashraf-ul Makhluqat'*, the noblest of all created objects, and also as the 'Vice-regent of God on Earth'.

Man, however, in his own way, began feeling an in-born urge for nearness to God, and has been ceaselessly in search of Him. Man has moved in many ways in search of God, some times losing direction and getting into wilderness, and some times turning towards the eternal Light in the process of approaching Divine Excellence.

Man's perception is impeded by limitations of faculties inherent in his physical senses. Human wisdom can not adequately comprehend the Sublimity and Majesty characterising the attributes of the Supreme Being, because such attributes are imponderable and incomprehensible for any human mind.

Being the compassionate Protector and Sustainer of all His creations, God has provided general benignity for all, but in respect of Man, the Crown of Creations, God has extended a special measure of benevolence, by providing divine guidance for the welfare of all men, of all Nations and at all times. Moreover, God has provided qualities of self-development for all the Creation, but man being gifted with reason and sense of discrimination, has received from God a further benevolent gift enabling him to attain nearness to the Throne of God.

Rabbil Alameen:

The notion of Qur'anic God, Allah, is uncompromisingly above any thing humanly comprehensible. Allah is not the same as conventional God or a fraternity of gods. Allah is the Creator, Sustainer and Protector of all mankind and of all forms of creation, the visible and the invisible, existing in the still expanding Cosmos, known and yet to be known.

The very opening sentence of the Holy Qur'an signifies Allah's identity as *'Rabbil Alameen'*, commonly translated as 'the Lord of the Worlds'. But this rendering is utterly inadequate. Maulana Abul Kalam Azad, in his erudite treaties *'Tarjuman al-Qur'an'* has attempted to clarify the notion of God *(Rabb)*, as envisaged in the Qur'an. The term *'Rabb'* is embellished by the combination of three divine attributes, namely, the Creator, the Nourisher and the Sustainer. To visualise God as Rabb, is to conceive of Him not only as the Creator of every thing in the Universe and beyond, but its Nourisher and Sustainer as well, providing sustenance appropriate to each object, and regulating with benignity its growth and development. The other portion of the expression *'Alameen'*, means not only the World or Worlds, but the entire Universe in its full cosmic proliferation. Thus the notion of Allah embraces the entire cosmic discipline, and of every thing that ever came to exist or is yet to be brought into existence in the process of limitless and unending expansion of His Creation.

Elucidating the theme, Maulana Azad says, "The provision that He has made for the sustenance and growth of every thing is made under a plan, so marvellous that every being is furnished with all that its particular nature demands for its existence, and at the same time, it is furnished in a manner that takes congnizance of every changing situation and need. The ants crawl on earth, the worms push their way in mud and dirt, the fish swim in water, the birds fly in air, the flowers blossom in gardens, the elephants wander in jungle and the stars revolve in the heavens. But on every one of these, rests the protecting eye of Providence, and there is none that is denied its blessings. Indeed, there are countless varieties of creation so infinitesimally small in form that our naked eye can not perceive them. For them also, the 'Rububiyat' of God has made the requisite provision for sustenance and growth with as much care as for the bulky elephant or the intelligent man" (R-1).

The instinctive behaviour of insects and other creatures such as the bee collecting honey, is not the result of blind choice, but of God's guidance through genetic impulse to perform those actions that are essential for their sustenance and survival. The Supreme Creator takes punctilious care even of the meanest and smallest of creatures that naked eye can not see. His divine Benevolence is equally extended over all categories of mankind - black, yellow or white, whether living under the hot Sun of the tropics or in the snowy blizzard of the Polar regions. Divine Benevolence is Universal.

Reference

R-1: *The Tarjuman al-Qur'an, Vol.I,* by Maulana Abul Kalam Azad, tr. by Dr. Syed Abdul Latif, 3rd Edition, Hyderabad, 1981: page 20.

Section III

GOD'S CHANGEFUL UNIVERSE

God is Changeless:

God, Whom we reverentially remember by the exalted appellation of *al-Hayy* and *al-Qayyum* (Ever-living and Eternal) is changeless. Changelessness or immutability is one of God's exclusive attributes. He has not vested this divine attribute on any of His creation, so that none can claim equality with Him by being immutable or changeless. If God wanted to make any of His countless creation changeless, any created object or even the Universe itself could have been made a changeless entity once for all by one single divine Command *'KUN'* ('Be'). Thereafter God could have gone to take an unending rest, or even could have ceased to exist. But His Universe is designed on a different concept. It is a changing Universe, requiring His all-pervading intensive attention at all times. His creation is ever growing, expanding, multiplying, diversifying, and ultimately changing to what pattern 'Man Knoweth Not'. No where is there any manifestation of changelessness or immutability.

Every Thing Else is Changeful:

God alone is changeless, every thing else in the Universe is changeful. A continual and comprehensive process of change is going on eternally with regard to the entire range of Creation from the Cosmos down to the core of the Earth. There is no exception.

Change is wedded to Time:

Change is an inescapable factor of Time. Where there is the flow of Time, there is the inevitability of Change. It is Time that changes infancy into old age, brings death if there is birth, causes ruin after flourish, and alternates rise with fall, prosperity with adversity. Change is the vary nature of Time.

Day changes into night. The Seasons change in the flight of Time. The Moon changes its phase every day. The Sun and the Earth are undergoing changes eternally, though imperceptibly for human eye. All of them are slaves of Time, and are changing at the bidding of Time.

Human Society is changing:

Human society, like the Universe itself, is growing and expanding. The rapidly proliferating Homo Sapiens are filling the sparseness of the Globe as a result of explosion of population, which in turn is compelling man's enterprise for moving into other Planets.

Man's Civilization is changing stage by stage. Emerging from a state of barbarism, the nomads took to settled Agriculture. Thereafter, the drift of Time resulted in the Agricultural Civilization to be dominated by the Industrial Era. The Industrial Era was also eclipsed with the march of Time, and was supplanted by Technological Revolution, which in turn is now threatened by a fresh concept of Cosmological adventure becoming feasible with the possibility of coming Space Age. Change after change is the unfailing characteristic of God's Creation.

Thus human society has always been governed by changing concept and practice. As Time passes, man's behaviour, personality and psychology are undergoing change at faster and accelerated rate. Until the 20th century, social change was so slow that it would pass unnoticed in one's life-time. That is no longer so. Now the quickening process of change has become a regular feature, posing a challenge to our imagination and capability.

Change is wholesale and continual:

A continual, all-pervading and comprehensive process of change is going on in God's eternal creation, covering all aspects of Time, Space and matter. Unfailing and persistent changes are occurring in the total complex of Natural phenomena, as well as in the realm of human society, whether in the sphere of Religion, Language, Customs or in the field of Thought and Action throughout the Ages since time immemorial.

The present Age however is unique in the context of incredible frequency of Change never experienced before. The sweep of Change is now beginning to come in all its vigour and vitality, and with inconceivable speed, demanding adaptation to new conditions at an equally fast pace. World communities of developed countries are some what aware of the possible dangers of Change, and are getting prepared to face them. The Muslim Community, however, does not appear alive to the inevitability of impending dangers. The community seems to have shut its eyes, as if it were possible to bypass the Inevitable by ignoring it.

Change in Divine Books:

The Eternal God is not subject to any change, but God's commands and even His Scriptures are prone to change in consonance with the flight of Time and change of circumstances. The various Scriptures of God, sent through different Prophets at different times for the guidance of mankind, are not identical, even though some of the under-lying principles may be broadly similar. There is no conformity in the Texts of different Divine Scriptures, namely, *Zaboor* (Psalms of David), *Taurat* (Old Testament of Moses), *Ingeel* (Bible of Jesus) and *al-Qur'an*, the last of the Revealed Books.

It may be that the first three Scriptures suffered from interpolations by human ingenuity and so their Texts and Teachings happened to vary widely. There was therefore the need and justification in rectifying the perversions and un-truths that had crept into these sacred books. The Holy Qur'an thereafter descended as a final measure of providing Divine Guidance for all mankind.

Change in Qur'anic Verses:

Al-Qur'an is God's words. God's words are not exactly the same in stature as God Himself. The Qur'an therefore can not claim parity with God. God is not changeable. The Qur'an can not vie with God in the matter of unchangeability. The Qur'an has been divinely subjected to some trifle changes at times, which is known as 'abrogation' or annulment of the Verses of the Qur'an.

The theory of Abrogation of Qur'anic Verses is not a subject of unanimous agreement among eminent scholars of Islamic Literature. Some scholars, particularly of the thinking of Maulana Muhammad Ali of Lahore, hold that there is no abrogation in the Qur'an. But most of the other scholars of high eminence are of the view that some of the Verses have been abrogated by Divine Command. Imam as-Suyuti, the celebrated Commentator of the Qur'an and Author of *'Itqan'* has taken great pains to critically examine and ennumerate the annulled Qur'anic Verses. He confirms that as many as 20 Verses of the Holy Qur'an have been withdrawn or substituted by Divine Revelation. (R-1).

A later Theologian and Spiritualist Shah Waliullah of Delhi mentions in his book *'Fauz-al Kabir'* that out of 20 cases of abrogation enlisted by Suyuti, there is firm proof of 5 Verses having been abrogated. These Verses are:

Surah Al-Baqarah, ayat 2:180 - It relates to bequeathing wealth for parents and relations.

Surah Al-Baqarah, ayat 2:240 - It prescribes maintenance for wives.

Surah Al-Anfal, Ayat 8:65 - It affirms that 20 patient Muslims are better than 200 others.

Surah Al-Ahzab, ayat 33:52 - It speaks about taking of wives.

Surah Al-Mujadilah, ayat 58:12 - It advises paying alms before meeting the holy Prophet.

The circumstances necessitating abrogation have not been stated by any Commentator. Maulana Ashraf Ali Thanavi, the noted Author of *'Behishty Zewar'*, writes in his *'Muqaddamah'* to the Holy Qur'an (R-2) that there are three categories of abrogated Verses of the Qur'an, and that Dua-i Qunut forms one of the instances of abrogation.

It is for men gifted with wisdom and insight to reflect upon the fact that after Revelation of a certain number of Qur'anic Verses, God chose to cancel them or replace them with better ones at some point of time. This is clear from *Surah Al-Baqarah, ayat 2:106*, wherein God says, "Such of Our Revelations as We abrogate or cause to be forgotten, We bring (in its place) one better or the like thereof. Knowest thou not that Allah is able to do all things?"

In the same way, God speaks of effecting changes in

revealed ayats in another instance. *Surah An-Nahl, ayat 16:101* says, "And when we put a Revelation in place of another Revelation - and Allah knoweth best what He revealeth".

It thus appears that the Qur'anic Verses, the highest form of God's Benevolence for guidance of mankind have been changed by God's own divine dispensation, according to the needs of the times and the inevitable changes of circumstances.

Change in Divine Commandments:

Whenever judged necessary due to passage of time or variation in circumstances, God decrees change in Divine Commandments. One such important change, for instance, may be seen in the change in location of *Qibla*. Literally, '*Qibla*' means any thing opposite. Opposite to the face of a Muslim engaged in the worship of Allah, is the venue of '*Qibla*' or the *Baitullah* the, House of God in the sacred City of Mecca. Its existence was recognised by an express injunction of the Qur'an contained in *Surah Al-Baqarah*, but the location was changed to *Baitul Muqaddas* in Jerusalam, and thereafter again to *Baitullah* in Mecca. The circumstances under which the changes occurred are mentioned below.

A reliable account of the change in the venue of *Qibla* comes from al-Baizawi, the noted Commentator of the Holy Qur'an, who says (R-3) that so long as the Prophet was in Mecca, the *Ka'bah* was regarded as the *Qibla*. After his migration to Medina, he was ordered by God to face the *as-Sakhrah*, a Mount at Jerusalem with a Temple at the top, which was treated as the *Qibla* by way of respect for sentiments of the Jews. About 16 months later, the Prophet desired to revert to the original *Qibla* at Mecca, and sought God's pleasure to sanctify it. The Prophet's Prayer was answered by revelation of relevant *ayats* in

Surah Al-Baqarah Nos. 2:142 and *144*. Thus the location and premises of Qibla was changed through Divine Revelation.

According to a traditional account, there was an occurrence in the second year of the Hijri Era. On one occasion, the holy Prophet was engaged in *Namaz Zuhr* in the outskirts of Medina, facing towards *Baitul Muqaddas.* In the midst of the *Namaz,* Angel Jibraeel appeared in vision and communicated the divine message that the direction of the Qibla is forthwith changed to *Baitullah* in Mecca. The Prophet at once implemented the Divine Command, by turning in the midst of the Prayer from the direction of Jerusalem, and completed the remaining portion of the *Namaz* facing towards Mecca. Ever since then, the *Qibla* has remained fixed at the same sacred spot, the *Baitullah* at Mecca. In memory of this historical event, the Mosque where the Prophet was offering prayers on that occasion, has been named *'Masjid-e Qiblatain'*, or the Mosque of double *Qiblas* located at a short distance from the city of Medina.

Change in Shariah Laws:

The Laws of Shariah have changed from country to country, and from time to time. They may undergo change in future, but only when there are valid reasons for bringing about a change. Some hard-liners argue that the Shariah is divinely inspired and no mortal can alter it. By saying so, they betray their ignorance of the history of Shariah Laws. The changes in Shariah can be brought about by the process of Ijma or through State Legislation to meet the genuine needs of the Community at a particular time. Sir D. F.Mulla, author of *'Principles of Mahomedan Law'* says, "The Hanafi Doctrine lays down that the provisions of Law must change with the change of time." The Maliki law makes it clear "that new facts require new decisions." (R-4)

Allah Favours Change:

Allah is not opposed to change under justifiable circumstances. Legitimate changes are welcome under provisions of the Holy Qur'an. *Surah Ar-Ra'd* says (13:11)

> "Verily Allah changeth not the condition of a people until they (first) change their conditions by themselves."

Islam can ensure its qualities of Universalism and perpetual freshness only through appropriate changes justified by passage of time and alteration in circumstances.

Conclusion:

So if every essential concept, every single entity of God's limitless Universe is subject to change, the decision of closure of the Door of Ijtihad can not be an exception.

Reference

R-1 : *Dictionary of Islam* by T.P. Hughes, Cosmo Publications, New Delhi, 1982, page 520.

R-2 : *'Aksi Qur'an Majeed Mutarjam,* with Urdu Translation and Commentary by Maulana Ashraf Ali Thanavi, Farid Book Depot, Delhi, page 3.

R-3 : *Dictionary of Islam* as at (R-1), page 480.

R-4 : *Mulla's Mahamedan Law,* 18th Edition, edited by Justice M. Hidayetullah, N. M. Tripathi, Bombay, page XXIV.

Section IV

ISLAMIC LAW AND ITS SOURCES

اَلْيَوْمَ اَكْمَلْتُ لَكُمْ دِيْنَكُمْ وَاَتْمَمْتُ عَلَيْكُمْ
نِعْمَتِيْ وَرَضِيْتُ لَكُمُ الْاِسْلَامَ دِيْنًا ط

Meaning- *"This day have I perfected your Religion for you, and completed My favours unto you, and have chosen for you al-Islam as Religion."*

-Holy Qur'an : *Surah al-Ma'idah* (5:3).

Al-Qur'an: The first Source of Islamic Law:

The Holy Qur'an, styled otherwise as 'Al-Furqan', stands as an Authority showing Truth from falsehood, and Right from wrong. The ideology of the Qur'an instils the spirit of Humanism, Tolerance and Universal Brotherhood among mankind. It conveys the eternal message of God for all times and all climes, which men and Jinn, whether singly or in collaboration, can never hope to emulate and produce even to the extent of one single Verse. Its Literature is noted for unrivalled elegance of style, diction and rhythmic cadence. Imam Jalaluddin as-Suyuti, Arabian Commentator, has enumerated 35 distinctive features pertaining to its literary excellence alone. Writers like Phillip K. Hitti, Charles Francis Potter and others, none of whom are known for their sympathetic approach to Islam, have acknowledged the fact that the Qur'an is "the most widely read book in existence" (R-1).

With all the above excellence, the Holy Qur'an is the first and primary source of Divine Islamic Law, descended by a process of Revelation for the guidance of human society. It is the infra-structure of Islamic legal system, and contains the basic principles on which the edifice of Islam is built.

Hadith - the second Source:

The next source of Islamic Laws is the holy Prophet's traditions - the Hadith or Sunnah, which were indispensable for interpretation, enlargement and elucidation of the under-lying principles of the Qur'an. It is the second footing in the structure of Islamic Laws. In its original sense, Hadith indicates the sayings and Sunnah refers to the doings of the holy Prophet, but in actual effect, both cover same ground of actions, practices and sayings of the Prophet. Memory was the chief means of their preservation, though some of them were occasionally recorded in writing.

In course of time, as the Muslim community rapidly grew and widely spread, it was necessary to collect and record the reliable incidents of Hadith. Ultimately, six Collections of Hadith known as 'SIHAH SITTA', took the codified form, out of which Sahih Bokhari has the unquestioned distinction of being the First.

Other Sources:

But even with the codification of Hadith, and with the positive provisions of the Qur'an, the Law did not suffice for the regulation of legal and social affairs of the rapidly growing community. The sweeping territorial expansion of Islam and the advancement in legal and administrative responsibilities created compelling necessity of taking decision on new aspects of life and activity, in which the Qur'an and Hadith did not indicate specific lines to follow. Where the law was not expressly stated to cover a particular case, an independent effort had to be made to find the correct answer.

It was under the circumstances necessary to evolve other ideologies compatible with the available first and second sources of Law. Incorporation of two new regulatory provisions, namely, Ijma (consensus) and Qiyas (analogy) was deemed expedient for completion of the structure of Islamic Law, even though intricate and bitter controversies kept on raging for some time around those two novel concepts.

Completion of Legal Structure:

The Islamic Law thus completed with the incorporation of Ijma and Qiyas, was totalitarian in form in the sense that it pervaded all aspects of life, and it assumed total authority over all activities of the Muslim community. Even then, there were some fields left open where the law did not impose restrictions. In some realms, it spoke absolutely, in others permissively.

The Islamic Law recognised and encouraged natural instincts of spiritual progress, material prosperity, universal fraternity and individual equality. Islam as a Religion, is optimistic and sanguine in its estimate of human nature, and its Laws are meant for regulating such a liberal society.

Shariah:

Muslim life is inalienably dependent upon the system known as Shariah. Literally, the term 'Shariah' means 'path' or 'mode'. When a man has faith on Allah, on His Prophet Hazrat Muhammad, on His holy Book the Qur'an, on the Angels and on the Day of Judgment *'Qiyamat'*, he is said to be a Believer, or a person having *'Iman'*. Thereafter, the mode in which he has to serve

Allah and the path he has to traverse in obeying Allah, is called *'Shariah'*. The mode and the path have been indicated by Allah through His Prophet Muhammad. But in course of time, some great Religious Teachers interpreted the holy Prophet's Shariah according to their own way of understanding. This led to division of Ummah into many sects, such as Hanafi, Maliki, Shafe'i, Hanbali, Ahl-e Hadith and so on. Each of them began to depend upon a set of Shariah, one slightly different from the other. But all of them acknowledge the Qur'an and Hadith as the final authority, and draw guidance therefrom according to their own way of thinking.

It is sensible to hold that any difference in the mode of serving God does not amount to deviation from Islamic path or *'Deen'*, provided the person concerned follows a particular mode (Shariah) after being genuinely conscious of the fact that Allah and His Prophet have actually laid down the line of action, and that he has made sincere and hard efforts to understand the Injunctions of the Qur'an and the precepts of Hadith in this regard.

In support of this view, Maulana Abul 'Ala Maududi says, "Every Muslim has the right to follow Shariah according to his sincere understanding and firm faith". (R-2).

IJMA - the Third Source:

"My Community will never unite in error".
- *Prophet Hazarat Muhammad*

The term 'Ijma' is derived from the root *Jam'*, which means 'collecting together' or 'uniting and agreeing in opinion together'. In the terminology of Muslim Jurists, Ijma means a consensus of opinion of the Mutahids, or an agreement of the Muslim Jurists of a particular age on a question of Law.

The newly emerging frame of mind ready to honour the general consensus of the Community led to a development whereby some type of general opinion or fresh decision acquired the force of Law which was considered as good as the authority of the divine Law. This turn of mind is an acknowledgment of the concept - "After God, the Prophet and thereafter the Community".

The concept of Ijma thus rested on the basis of consensus of the community. The general principle is that Truth is secured in the wider range of mind of the community. As there is the risk of an individual or a smaller group to go astray, reliance should be placed on the decision of the community at large. The Muslim community as a whole is not likely to go far into a position which may turn out to be wrong from Islamic point of view.

Ijma should not however be equated with democratic law, as it is not born of the majority opinion statistically determined. There is some subtlety in the notion of Ijma. It is first of all, the exposition of a common elevated mind on a particular point, giving legal recognition to an existing shade of opinion which has come to favour in the mind of the Community. Secondly, while the Qur'an and Hadith may be silent on the point at issue, the decision is not repugnant to any Injunction of the sacred Scriptures.

Some Schools of Thought have differed profoundly on the quality and sanctity of consensus leading to Ijma. Even among some pious minded intellectuals, the concept of Ijma has created mental conflict. But on the whole, there is no overall reluctance to accept Ijma. Many among learned and pious minds have accepted its sanctity. Its operation has resulted in creating a fresh lot of Laws, just as binding as those coming from the Scriptures. Ijma thus acquired the recognition of the third Foundation of Islamic Laws.

Ijma is a valid feature of Law observed by all the four Sunni Sects, though the Rules deduced from Ijma have varying degrees of sanctity in different Schools of Thought. The Hanafis regard Ijma as a fundamental source of Law, but the Shafe'is regard it as of minor importance. The Malikis place Ijma of Medinese Ulama above the Ijma of all others. The Hanbalis accept only the Ijma of the Sahaba, and not of any body else. The Wahabis therefore reject the Ijma of all later generation. Among the Shi'as, the Ijma of the present day Mujahideen is freely accepted. They do not accept the closure of the Gate.

The Hanafi Muslims have laid down degrees of importance according to the status of Scholars who contributed to the formulation of the particular Ijma. They serialise the sanctity of Ijma according to the following order:

(i) Ijma of Sahaba;
(ii) Ijma of the Jurists;
(iii) Ijma of Mujtahid's opinion on new problems;
(iv) Ijma on which there were earlier dissent by some Mujtahids, and later there was the consensus.

There is some diversity of opinion regarding upto what period in the History of Islam, Ijma was valid. Some scholars are of the opinion that only the Ijma of Mujtahids who were *Ashab* (Companion of the Prophet) can be strictly regarded as valid. Other Scholars hold in varying degrees the Ijma of the *Tabi'in* (those who conversed with the Companions), the *Ansars* (the helpers living in Medina), the *Muhajireen* (those who accompanied the Prophet in his Hijrat to Medina), and the *Taba'ut Tabi'in* (the followers of the *Tabi'in*) to be quite valid as the third step in the structure of Islamic Laws.

It is also held that "One Ijma may be replaced by another Ijma in the same age or in the subsequent age, with the reservation that the Ijma of the Companions of the holy Prophet can not be reversed by any later generation." (R-3).

Under modern conditions of life, it is not practically possible to carry out the operation of Ijma as it is understood in orthodox sense. The idea has been explicitly cleared by Maulana Muhammad Ali of Lahore, who says, "If Ijma is taken to mean the consensus of opinion of all the Mujtahids of a certain generation of Muslims, it has never been practicable after perhaps the early days of the Companions of the holy Prophet. The Muslims having spread far and wide, and living as they did in distant places, could not all be occupied with the discussion of a certain question at one and the same time. Even in one country, the same question need not occupy the attention of all the Mujtahids simultaneously". (R-4).

The above views of Maulana Muhammad Ali are supported by a distinguished Author of Islamic Culture, Dr. Fazlur Rahman of Lahore, who in his book 'Islamic Methodology in History' sharply criticises the classical views of orthodox Scholars confining the operation of Ijma within unbending and rigid limits. Dr. Rahman says that the concept of Ijma is not static and bckward-looking, but is distinctly forward-looking, ever expanding and is "utterly democratic in temper".(R-5)

A modern Pakistani Author of repute, Dr. Ahmad Hasan, Professor of Islamic Research Institute of Islamabad, has elaborately dealt with the Juridical Principles of Ijma in his learned book 'The Doctrine of

Ijma in Islam'. His views may best be presented by giving relevant extracts from the last few pages of the book as below:

"The Classical Theory portrays Ijma as a total agreement of the Community or of the Scholars. The classical Jurists dilated on it with all its implications. They raised important questions with regard to its conception, definition, competence, period, procedure and applicability, and sought to present the Theory in its complete form."

"There are, however, a number of points that are lacking in the Classical Theory. The most significant of them is the absence of a machinery for its practical functioning. The Classical Theory presents Ijma as a purely informal activity of the Scholars in their private and individual capacity with no definite organisation and specific procedure. Further it is content to describe certain qualifications for the competence of Ijma; it does not identify the persons in whom these qualifications were actually found, and who could be considered competent for it in its true sense. The condition of 'total agreement' of the Scholars has again been condemned by the opponents. The unanimous agreement of the community is confined to the essentials of Religion. The consensus of the Scholars has been presented as the Ijma of the community. This has also not been universally recognised. Those who defined it as an agreement of the whole Community, like Al-Ghazali, were severely criticised by the Classical Jurists. A large number of questions concerning points of detail are said to have been covered by Ijma. Such questions are in fact, supported by tacit Ijma communicated verbally. The validity of the tacit Ijma is already disputed. The most objectionable point that strikes the modern mind is that the Classical Theory neglects in Ijma the intellectual elite and the masses which constitute the bulk of the community. In certain situations the masses and the public opinion practically bypass the agreements of the Scholars, and the Scholars themselves recognise it with the passage of time by their practice. Can it be charcterised as Ijma? The objections raised by the exponents of Ijma themselves, let alone the opponents, indicate that the Classical Theory of Ijma was not recognised in full even during its formative period. Because of its purely theoretical nature and perhaps for want of some definite practical machinery it could not be utilised to reform the Muslim Society. "

"The Doctrine of Ijma, of course, played a fundamental and significant role in conserving the past heritage and formation of Institutions in Islam. It served as a unifying force, like some parallel institutions of other Religions, in the Muslim community. It engendered unity and solidarity in the whole system of law, dogma and rituals. Creating unity in diversity was the principal function of Ijma in the medieval times. And probably for this purpose this principle, though forward-looking and progressive in its early stages, was theorised in a retrospective manner and it went a long way towards fulfillment of this objective."

"It seems that the concept of Ijma originally began as a theory of the will of the community. This theory continued for a certain period of time until the rise of Scholars as a pressure group in the Muslim society. With their dominance in religious sphere, and with the separation of religion from politics in practice, the Scholars were regarded as representing the will of the community. Another reason may be that the Ulama in the medieval times almost constituted the whole of the educated class and the intellectual elite of the society. The masses mostly relied on them in different matters, specially in religious affairs. The consciousness of common men in the affairs of society, whether religious, political or social, grew fast in modern times. Allegiance to a single authority, a chief characteristic of the medieval period, was replaced by allegiance to the public will. Hence the modern mind is not covinced of the classical definition of Ijma which shows the hierarchy of the Scholars in Islam. Modernists seek to employ it as a 'tool of reform'. Influenced by the universal democratic trend in thinking, they identify public opinion, public will, opinion of the intellectual elite of the society, and the enactments of representative assemblies of the Muslim countries with the Ijma of the community. There are of course people who take it only as a unifying and conserving authority. They see little hope of reform through Ijma in view of its classical definition."

"We think the Ulama or the specialists provoke public opinion to form a consensus on a given question by their expert opinion. And if they are agreed, it certainly constitutes Ijma, though only tentatively, unless it is confirmed by the will of the community, i.e. by practically recognising or rejecting it in course of time. The Classical theory recognises the opinion of the masses and intellectuals only in respect of essentials or in questions directly relating to them. But it recognises the consensus of the Scholars alone on questions of purely academic and technical nature. The masses do not come into the picture. We are of the view that even on such questions, the Ijma of the Scholars may be accepted in a tentative manner to be finally approved of by the will of the Community at large."

"In the present political situation, the division of the Muslim Community into a number of National States has created fresh problems for the formation of Ijma. There are problems which are of purely religious nature, and require the assent of the universal community. Others relate to a local situation obtaining in a Muslim country. What should be the procedure of reaching Ijma on both these types of questions? We are of opinion that questions of universal nature may be discussed on international level in a meeting of experts who represent different Muslim countries. The consensus arising out of their deliberations may form a tentative Ijma of a functional nature. It will be regarded as permanent when confirmed by the universal community. As to the Ijma on questions of parochial nature, the specialists or elite of the society, as the case may be, of a particular Muslim Country may form a consensus, by their mutual discussion, say, in a National Assembly, which will be of a temporary nature. This can be confirmed or rejected in course of time by the will of the local community. It is worthy of remark that both types of Ijma, local and universal, will function as a temporary measure, subject to the acceptance or rejection by the universal or local community in the long run."

"Ijma, it may be noted, is not retrospective by nature as the classical theory depicts it. Originally it started as a forward-looking and prospective phenomenon. Modern researches of the early period show that Ijma in pre-Shafe'i period was an on-going process, liable to be changed with the change of conditions. It exercised a check against the fallibility of new content which emerged in the wake of Ijtihad-Ijma activity. With the cessation of original thinking in Law and suspension of the activity of Ijtihad, it became inert by degrees, and ultimately a custodian of tradition. But it can be utilised for the benefit of Muslim society by taking it back to its original conception."(R-6).

It seems reasonable to hold that when a particular tenet of Islam appears to have become impracticable, it may not always be due to any shortcoming in the tenet, but to the way in which the tenet is interpreted at that particular point of time. So if any particular Doctrine of Ijma appears to have lost its relevance at the present time, an effort should be made to interpret it sensibly, instead of putting the whole principle in the cold storage.

QIYAS - the Fourth Source:

Imam Ash-Shafe'e, the founder of the Shafe'i School of Jurisprudence, was the originator of the Doctrine of Qiyas, even though the first cue came from Imam Abu Hanifa.

The concept of Qiyas rested on the principle of extension of fundamental Islamic Law on the basis of similarity in two situations, one of which was specifically provided in the Qur'an or Hadith. The other situation was reasonably inferred from the first. For instance, the Qur'an prohibited the taking of wine. On the strength of Qiyas, the prohibition also extended to other intoxicants which had deleterious effect. The exponents of Qiyas were required to justify the appropriateness of the analogy between the two situations of objects under consideration.

The justification of the analogy was based on the method of resolving new issues in the light of pre-existing rulings or precedents compared with the circumstances of the new situation. In some cases, the new issues could be settled in the light of directions of the Qur'an or Hadith, through the process of deductive-inductive interpretation. Secondly, a relevant provision in the sacred literature may be searched by intellectual efforts, and its parallelism established with the new situation. Where the two are of the same quality and nature, the existing principle may be applied to the new issue. This process of equating the past precedent and the present issue is the basis of the principle of Qiyas.

When Qiyas was first declared as a valid form of Shariah, there was strong reaction, because the new provision was deemed to involve the risk of taking the mind of the people away from the original sayings and doings of the Prophet. The dangers arising from the justification behind the analogy led to difference of opinion among Scholars. As a result, the principle of Qiyas did not attain popularity in subsequent times.

Reference

R-1 : *Tafsir-ul Qur'an,* by Maulana Abdul Majid Daryabadi, (Lucknow, Vol.I, page ix)

R-2 : *Fundamentals of Islam* by Maulana Abul 'Ala Maududi, (Delhi, page 84).

R-3 : *The Religion of Islam* by Maulana Muhammad Ali, (S. Chand & Co., New Delhi, 1981, page 108)

R-4 : Ibid page 109).

R-5 : *Islamic Methodology in Histrory* by Dr. Fazlur Rehman, (Lahore, 1965, Pages 6, 20, 24).

R-6 : *The Doctrine of Ijma in Islam* by Dr. Ahmad Hasan, Islamic Research Institute, Islamabad, Pakistan, 1984, pages 259-61).

Section V

IJTIHAD

The Theory:

The Holy Qur'an is the embodiment of Divine Wisdom necessary for the guidance of mankind: mankind which is destined to live from Age to Age, and spread from country to country, and rule over God's creation all the time. In order to be worthy of playing such a potential role, Man was required to exert himself for continuous advancement along the right path.

Apart from the counsel to exert, the Qur'an abounds in exhortations to mankind to take resort to Reason and exercise of Judgment. It appeals and urges by repeated injunctions, 'use your eyes and ears, your minds and hearts, your powers of reason and judgment. For, those who fail to do so are worse than beasts.' There are also inspiring interrogations, "Do you not reflect?" "Do you not understand?", "There are signs in this phenomenon for men of Wisdom", etc.

The holy Prophet earnestly gathered the essence of these Qur'anic persuations, and formulated them into a principle known in Juristic language as 'Ijtihad'. This was done with the utmost wisdom and foresight, so that Islam may be able to maintain its character of Universalism by enabling the Ummah to adjust themselves from Age to Age according to the requirements of ever changing conditions of the World.

Ijtihad Defined:

The term 'Ijtihad' is derived from the root *'Jehd'*,

meaning exerting oneself to the utmost. Ijtihad is a Doctrine which implies the exercise of one's utmost reason to deduce a principle compatible with the Shariah. The injunctions of the Qur'an and the precepts of Hadith are the elementary sources of Islamic Law. Where the Scriptural texts are silent and do not cover a new situation, an independent effort is called for as a result of compelling necessity to lay down the line of action. As a measure of foresight, the principle of Ijtihad was devised to provide for accommodation of future needs, so that new rulings might be formulated in cases where no specific Law existed in the Qur'an and Hadith.

The Qur'an's pre-eminent message is spiritual and ethical, though it also serves to an extent as a worldly guide. The Holy Book was not intended to be a complete Code of Law, although it embodies a number of rudimentary legal provisions. Hadith however, covers more elaborate legal provisions which also are comprehensive. In actual life and activity, the people had the necessity of more extensive legal Code, which became all the more pressing as new situations arose with the rapid territorial expansion of the Islamic Empire. Ijtihad was called into service to meet the growing legal requirements of the expanding Commonwealth of Muslims.

Growth and Expansion:

The actual operation of the principle of Ijtihad was started by the holy Prophet himself. As it was not possible that all cases arising within the fold of the growing Muslim population should be referred to the Prophet, the Companions used to operate the principle as occasion arose from time to time. After the Prophet's death, as new areas were added to the growing Empire of Islam, the practice of Ijtihad spread over vast territory and occurred with greater frequency. The four Khulafa-e Rashideen, particularly Hazrat Umar resorted to Ijtihad quite frequently. Besides, some great learned individuals such as Hazrat A'isha, Ibn Abbas, Ibn Umar and others also worked as wise and respected authority for formulating principles of Ijtihad, taking care that their decisions were not contrary to the Injunctions of the Qur'an and Sunnah.

THE SOURCES OF IJTIHAD

Primary Source - the Qur'an:

The concept of Ijtihad had its origin in a well-known Verse of the Holy Qur'an in Surah Al-Ankabut (29:69), which reads as follows-

وَالَّذِيْنَ جَاهَدُوْا فِيْنَا لَنَهْدِيَنَّهُمْ سُبُلَنَا ط

meaning, *"As for those who strive in Us,*
We surely guide them to our path."

In this sacred Verse, the Holy Qur'an has provided a sound foundation of the principle of Ijtihad to meet the growing legal requirements of the society in future. The Qur'an contains some basic principles for the regulation and guidance of a well-ordered society. At places, it contains a few detailed legal provisions, but mostly it reveals rudiments of principles, subject to elucidation and elaboration of foundational tenets. The intention is that the process of inference and deduction may be employed to meet the diverse needs of ever-growing life in a developing society in future. The potentiality of rudimentary Qur'anic principles is of such nature that all future problems of human society could be solved by evolving guiding Rules therefrom through inference and logical deduction.

In addition to the above-mentioned Ayat in *Surah Ankabut*, there are other Surahs in the Qur'an which recognise and encourage the exercise of Judgment with a view to search out correct Knowledge and arrive at sound decisions.

> *Surah 'An-Nisa'* lays down (4:83)-
> *"And when there comes to them tidings of safety or fear, they spread it all round, whereas if they had referred it to the Prophet and to such other persons as are in authority - those among them who can search out the Knowledge of it, would have known it".*

The Qur'anic term used in this Verse is *'Yastambitun'* derived form *'Istimbat'*, which literally means 'deduction', or 'drawing conclusion'. The jurists however use it to mean 'searching out hidden meaning'. Another term used in this verse is *Ulu'l-amr*, meaning men who are in authority, or who are in a position to search out the knowledge.

The Verse establishes the concept of *'Istimbat'*, which in turn serves as the foundation of the principle of Ijtihad. The meaning, as mentioned before, is exerting oneself to the utmost by exercise of Judgment in the process of searching out the underlying correct position, not incompatible with Shariah.

The Qur'an, while thus encouraging the process of Ijtihad, indicates that the function should be carried out by the Prophet and by *Ulu'l-amr*, men in authority. In another Verse in *Surah Al-e Imran (3:190-91)*, men who may be depended upon have been named as *Ulu'l-albab*, meaning men of wisdom and understanding. It is obvious that after the life time of the Prophet, the function of Ijihad is intended to be carried on by men of authority, power, wisdom and understanding.

The Next Source - Hadith:

Ijtihad is expressly recognised in Hadith as the means by which a decision may be arrived at, when there is no specific direction in the Qur'an or Hadith. The following

Hadith is regarded as the basis of Ijtihad in Islamic Jurisprudence:

On being appointed as the Governor of Yemen, Mu'az was asked by the Prophet, "O Mu'az, by what Rule you would be guided?". He replied, "By the Law of the Qur'an". "But if you find no direction therein?", asked the Prophet. "Then I will act according to the Sunnah of the Prophet", replied Mu'as. "But what if that also does not help?", he was again asked. "Then I will exercise my Judgement and act accordingly", was the reply. The Prophet raised his hands in satisfaction and thankfulness to God and uttered, "Praise be to Allah, Who guides the Messenger of His Apostle as He pleases". (R-1)

This Hadith shows that the holy Prophet approved of the principle of Ijtihad involving exercise of one's own Judgment when there are no specific direction in the Qur'an or the Sunnah. It further shows that the Prophet's Companions were aware of the principle, and that Ijtihad by other men in Prophet's life-time was freely resorted to when necessary in order to meet new circumstances.

It was the holy Prophet's sagacity in formulating the principle of Ijtihad that led to rapid and systematic development of Islamic law during and after his life-time.

Khulafa-e Rashideen and Ijtihad:

The work of Ijtihad had begun in the Prophet's life time. As it was not practically possible to refer all cases to the Prophet, the Companions and other 'men in authority' began to take resort to Ijtihad under justifiable circumstances.

Hazrat Abu Bakr invariably consulted the Qur'an and then Sunnah, and last of all he would gather together the best of the people for consultation on new type of problems, and would take the final decision according to the majority opinion. The same procedure was followed by Hazrat Umar, who resorted to Ijtihad freely, taking care to consult the most learned Companions. There were highly respected individual Teachers and Mujtahids who used to cite precedents or give decisions. The decisions of these Mujtahids were followed by later Jurists as long as they were not in disagreement with the Book of God and Sunnah.

Four Imams and Ijtihad:

In the second Century Hijri and thereafter, came the four great Jurist-Imams, namely:

Imam-e Azam Abu Hanifa : 80-150 AH (699-767 AD)

Imam Malik Ibn Anas : 94-179 AH (716-795 AD)

Imam Ibn Idris al-Shafe'i : 150-204 AH (767-820 AD)

Imam Ahmad Ibn Hanbal : 164-241 AH (780-856 AD)

All the four Imams agreed to uphold the sanctity of Ijtihad as an important source of Islamic law, and codified the Laws accordingly. In accepting a particular law as valid, Abu Hanifa applied reasoning very frequently and sought to deduce all questions from the holy Qur'an on the basis of Reason, as enough Hadith were not available at Kufa where he lived mostly. Imam Malik confined himself wholly to Hadith prevalent in Medina and applicable to the people of the city. Imam Shafe'i based his set of Laws mostly on Hadith, differing from the Hanafi System in the sense that the latter is based mostly on the Qur'an combined with reason. Imam Hanbal made very little use of reason and depended almost wholly on Hadith, even though most of the narrations were weak and not acceptable.

Deterioration in Standard:

In the process of Law-making, there was a gradual decline in standard, from the high ideals of the first Imam to the indiscriminate collection of Law by the last Imam. But with regard to the high standard of Imam Abu Hanifa, deterioration crept in as the later jurists of that School failed to develop the outlook and talent necessary to grasp the implications of the great Imam's thoughts. The result was the growing stagnation in the field of application and interpretation of Islamic Law.

Due to such deterioration in the quality of Law, the sanctity of Ijtihad was sought to be protected by classifying the collected materials into three levels. The first degree of Ijtihad was accorded to the work of the four Imams. The second degree was vested on the work of the immediate disciples of the four Imams. Imam Abu Yusuf and Imam Muhammad, the two famous disciples of Imam Abu Hanifa are honoured as the Mujtahids of the second degree. Later Jurists, who handled special cases not decided by the Mujtahids of the first and second degrees, were treated as authors of Ijtihad of the third degree.

Effects of Deterioration:

The classification of Ijtihad Legists into three degrees produced mixed results, good and bad. There may be sense in saying that when the Imam's Ijtihad gets first degree, the Ijtihad of his disciples should get second degree. But it is worth bearing in mind that Mujaddids were expected to appear at every turn of the Century, and it may be possible that a Mujaddid of a later Century may attain greater eminence than his old time compatriot. If so, it may be wrong to deny his Ijtihad the status of first degree. Mujaddid-e Azam Imam Ghazali was born more than 200 years after the death of the last of the four great Imams. It will be injustice to accord third degree to the ijtihad of Imam Ghazali.

Secondly, the effect of denial of first two degrees to later Jurists was that they felt frustrated and disappointed, as they could not hope for a high degree even if they happened to outshine the Scholars of earlier Age. In addition to such frustration, there was the general decline in intellectual level in and after the 4th Century Hijri, resulting in growth of inferiority complex among the later Scholars.

CATEGORIES OF IJTIHAD

The field of Ijtihad is extensive as it seeks to cover all legal requirements of Muslims not specifically indicated in the Qur'an and Hadith. Persons engaged in Ijtihad in earlier times made serious efforts in admitting and resolving new legal propositions by appropriate methods suited to each individual case. There are four such methods, namely, Qiyas (analogy), Istihsan (equity), Istislah (public interest), and Istidlal (rational custom).

Qiyas (Analogy):

The theory of Qiyas, broadly indicated by its English equivalent 'Analogy', is based on similarity in two situations considered in resolving new issues in the light of existing rulings of precedents. The meaning and implications of the theory are given in details in the previous Section IV.

Istihsan (Equity):

Imam Abu Hanifa and some renowned Jurists held that issues not covered by the Qur'an or Sunnah, may be resolved by the process of Ijtihad, based not on analogy but on consideration of public good or public justice. The

Hanafi Jurists laid down that whenever analogy failed to justify the requirements of public facility, the Jurists were at liberty to adopt a special rule conducive to public good, justice or convenience, and to give a shape to Ijtihad accordingly. They hold that this principle is in accordance with the spirit of the Qur'an. There is lesser liability to error in this method than in analogy, which often becomes far-fetched and ridiculous, and which some times leads to narrow results opposed to the broad spirit of the Qur'an. There was however some opposition from schools other than Hanafi. Ultimately, the system did not develop to the full extent.

Istislah (Public Interest):

This doctrine was developed by Imam Malik. It means a deduction of law based on the consideration of public interest. It was almost parallel to the system of Istihsan of Imam Abu Hanifa.

Istidlal (Rational Customs):

This is a system drawn from prevailing customs, usages and from the Laws of Religions revealed before Islam. It was agreed that the customs and usages obtaining in Arabia prior to the advent of Islam which were not declared abolished, have the force of good laws. On the same principle, the customs and usages of countries other than Arabia, when not expressly forbidden by the Qur'an, would also be admissible as good law. In fact, customs recognised by a vast majority of people are as good as Ijma, and hence they have precedence over a rule derived on the basis of analogy. The Hanafi Law lays special stress on the value of customs and usages which are considered rational.

The disciplines established by the four Imams hold divergent views on the principles of Ijtihad. But in spite of the apparent differences, the Hanafi, the Maliki and the Shafe'i Schools are agreed on broadening the original provisions of Fundamental Laws. The Istihsan of Abu Hanifa, the Istislah of Imam Malik and the Qiyas of Imam Shafe'i were intended to expand and liberalise the original legal tenets. Only Imam Hanbal is an exception who stuck to rigidity and did not accept the principle of Ijtihad. But in his own way, he softened the implications of Hadith by formulating the doctrine of 'Usul'

Ijtihad is not Infallible:

No Jurist can claim infallibility. As such, no Ijtihad can be treated as infallible, that is, not liable to error. Maulana Muhammad Ali says, "It is a recognised principle of Ijtihad that the Mujtahid may err in his judgment. Hence it is that so many differences of Juristic deductions exist even among the highest authorities. From its very nature, the Qiyas of one generation may be rejected by a following generation". (R-2).

Similarly, an Ijtihad decision reached a thousand years ago in Arabia may not necessarily be held valid in India today in view of considerable change in social and political factors and extensive widening of knowledge in the past thousand years.

In the second Century Hijri, the four great Imam-Mujtahids gave to the Islamic World their systems of Jurisprudence, each one differing from the other. Imam Malik did not accept all that his great predecessor Imam Abu Hanifa had said, nor did Imam Shafe'i agree with what his two predecessors had done. Although the first three Imams had practically exhausted the scope of Islamic Jurisprudence, Imam Hanbal further gave to the World the result of his vast learning and knowledge. No one of the four Imams considered the other as infallible.

If these great and eminent leaders of Islamic World were not infallible, no later Jurist can claim infallibility. The findings of Ijtihad are therefore liable to err, and they require to be checked and corrected if necessary by subsequent Ijtihads. If the door of Ijtihad is closed, the errors will remain unchecked and uncorrected for ever.

Reference

R-1 : *Dictionary of Islam* by Thomas Patrick Hughes (Cosmos Publications, New Delhi, 1982, page 198).

R-2 : *The Religion of Islam* by Maulana Muhammad Ali (S.Chand & Co., New Delhi, page 104).

Section VI

TAQLID

Extraneous Influence:

The Holy Qur'an, as revealed to the Prophet, came down to the first generation of Muslims with all the simplicity and pristine purity of Thought and Language. After about a Century, the influence of Greek thought began to creep into the mind of learned men engaged in preparation of commentaries to the Qur'an. The tendency of writing commentaries under extraneous influence grew in course of time as new Races got into the fold of Islam, bringing with them the heritage of their former faiths. The impact was particularly noteworthy in infusing anthropomorphic notions into the Islamic concept of Divinity, and in inducting a spirit of mysticism into the thought system of Islam. The result was seen in the development of a new approach to the style of interpretation, quite alien to the original ideology of the Qur'an.

The Doctrine:

By the 4th Century Hijri, a reaction started in order to stop foreign influence and innovations of all varieties. A hypothetical limit was fixed in thought and action in all spheres of life and work. People could look back to precedents and act accordingly, but could not advocate any new style of conduct in thinking and acting. This gave rise to the concept of 'Taqlid', which means 'imitation' or 'following'. It gradually developed into a form of doctrine, which degenerated into an attitude of thoughtless veneration for past traditions without any intellectual effort to assess its sanctity or relevance. It is a form of obscurantism which was committed to rigid adherence to medievalism in thought and action.

There was yet another factor responsible for growing allegiance to Taqlid. Sufism, in its spirit of other-worldliness and with its feature of high speculative thoughts, attracted and absorbed the best minds and brains of Islam during the Medieval times. The State administration was then left in the hands of second rate intellectuals. Under the circumstances, the unthinking mass of Muslims, having no other personalities of higher calibre to guide them, found their security only in following blindly the sectarian beliefs and practices based on the principles of Taqlid. Thus Taqlid got itself established gradually but firmly in the Socio-Religious disposition of the Muslim community. The doctrine continues to be in vogue in some sections of Muslim population till this day. It is sarcastically called 'Blind Faith'.

Taqlid is just the opposite of Ijtihad in the sense that Taqlid amounts to acceptance with full faith of the interpretations of Religion, Ethics, Philosophy and Tradition as advocated by the older generation of Jurists, who claimed their views to be authoritative and infallible, and did not tolerate the examination of the authenticity of such views by any body, while Ijtihad is an individual's own views arrived at after maximum efforts to weigh the juristic soundness of the proposition, which proposition shall not be repugnant to the provisions of the Qur'an and Hadith. Taqlid aims at holding Laws in a rigid mould, because it is believed that there is the stamp of divine approval upon such Laws, while Ijtihad aims at contributing freshness of thought to the concept, upholding universalism of Islamic values and making subject matters compatible with the requirements of modern life.

Muqallid:

The Muqallid is a person guided by faith on the Doctrine of Taqlid. Men with such faith hold that only the Faqihs of early Centuries of Islam possessed the real perspicuity and learning to deduce the relevant Fiqh from Divine Tenets embodied in the Qur'an and Hadith, and to prescribe them as infallible Laws for the guidance of Islamic Society. The Muqallid believe that no one else in the later Ages is capable of such performance with equal degree of talent and sanctity. They look down upon all innovations and fresh interpretations, even though they have no objections to admit interpretations made in the second Century Hijri under extraneous influence.

Opposition to Taqlid:

Opposition to Taqlid is as old as the Doctrine of Taqlid itself, but it grew slowly. By the 13th Century A.D., the refutation of the Doctrine became vocal and pronounced. Progressive trends in Islamic Law and its liberalisation, in fact, are wanted by men who are larger in number than those who want to resist them. But the progressive elements are mostly passive and do not back up their ideals by active efforts to create wide consensus. As the old-moded thinkers are generally vociferous about their views, and the Liberals simply welcome but do not physically assert in fulfilment of their aims, a false notion has come to stay that Taqlid has a larger supporting base.

Scholars strongly decrying the Doctrine of Taqlid are large in number and belong to different periods of History. A few cases are mentioned below:

(i) *Hafiz Ibn Taimiyah* (died 1283 AD) condemned Taqlid in his voluminous writings and extensive preachings. He deplored that Taqlid had made Muslims so degenerate and intolerant that the Founder of Madrasah Rawahiya of Damascus who was a Shafe'ite, considered the followers of Imam Hanbal as much outside the bounds of Islam as the Jews and Christians were.

(ii) *Shah Waliullah Mohaddis Dehlavi* (died 1763 AD) has mentioned in his books 'Izalah' and 'Hujjah' that the dying away of the spirit of Ijtihad led to domination of Taqlid, by which the minds of people were fettered by rigid conformity resulting in narrow outlook. He observed that only the thoughtless men take resort to Taqlid.

(iii) *Jamaluddin Afghani* (died 1897), who is noted for leading pan-Islamic Movement, was opposed to Taqlid, as well as to Theological hair-splitting and static religious piety totally divorced from contemporary conditions of life and work. He pressed for fresh investigation into the original sources of Islamic Law.

(iv) *Muhammad Abduh* (died 1950), the Egyptian Reformer and Commentator of Qur'an, worked for weakening the hold of rigid traditions upon Arab mind, and advocated adaptation to modern needs. He held that Taqlid was against the spirit of Islam.

(v) *Justice Syed Ameer Ali,* Author of 'The Spirit of Islam' and other well-known Islamic Literature, says that the Qur'an's spirit is in conformity with the progressive demands of Humanity, and that Taqlid is against such a sacred spirit.

(vi) *Sir Muhammad Iqbal (died 1938 AD),* in his famous book, 'The Reconstruction of Religious Thought in Islam', refers to the Qur'anic Ayat in *surah Ankabut (29:69),* forming the basis of Ijtihad as distinguished from Taqlid. In his diagnosis of weakness of Islam, he has identified uncritical veneration of the past as the true cause of the decline of Muslims, and has called for a new dynamism to reconstruct Religious Thought in Islam.

The above list of scholars opposed to Taqlid is not exhaustive. In fact, there are countless Muslim Intellectuals, with Western as well as Arabic Education, who are sharply critical of the role that the Doctrine of Taqlid has played in killing the urge for creativity and advancement by inducing baneful reverence for imitation of the past. They hold that Taqlid is against the spirit of the Qur'an, and have strongly advocated that the Doctrine be ignored, so that Muslims may depend upon Reason and Judgment, as exhorted repeatedly by the Holy Book.

Taqlid is Dogmatic:

The Scholars who believe in and preach the doctrine of Taqlid, think that the use of Reason and Judgment amounts to heresy; that Ijtihad is a kind of anti-Religious Secularism; that Taqlid is the only system which guarantees purity of Faith, and that departure from Taqlid amounts to abandonment of Islam. They are too authoritative, some times fanatical bigots, and they claim to possess the monopoly of Religious Thought and Wisdom, looking down on persons who are not of their way of thinking.

Taqlid acts as opium, goads men into inactivity, kills their initiative and leaves them without any constructive programme. Taqlid does not help to attain spiritual salvation or gain earthly advancement, but pushes men into social degeneration, economic decline and communal fanaticism.

If the interpretation of Scriptural Texts and legal provisions is left to the discretion of such imbalanced dogmatists, intellectual growth will be arrested and spiritual attainment mis-directed, while ignorance, obsoletism and superstition will take over the heart and soul of the Muslim community.

Section VII

CLOSING THE GATE

Prosperous Ijtihad Era:

During the first three Centuries of the Hijri Calendar, a host of eminent Religious Leaders appeared on the scene, and took frequent resort to the process of Ijtihad when necessary, thereby providing solution to a multitude of Socio-Religious problems of countries and races that had merged with the growing Islamic Commonwealth. Ijtihad served as a source of great blessings for the country and the people, and heralded the events that contributed to the Golden Age of Islam. As a result, there was enormous progress and prosperity in all spheres of life. All branches of Science, Arts, Literature, Philosophy and cultural enterprises kept on flourishing with tremendous vigour and vitality.

Change in Outlook:

At the dawn of the 4th Century Hijri, the temper of Times began to show signs of change. Reaction set in, and the pendulum of thought and action swung to the other side. The Age of brilliant Jurists had come to an end with the demise of the last of the Faqihs and Mohaddisain. The Scholars of the succeeding generation who then appeared on the scene, could not be expected to match or out-shine the talent of Jurists of the 2nd and 3rd Centuries Hijri. The four great Imams particularly had risen so high above the other Jurists of the time that every body was paled into insignificance. There was therefore the inevitable feelings of frustration resulting in marked decline in talent in later times.

To cover up these failings and frustrations, a new question was raised--if Ijtihad was a continuous and ever-lasting process, open as a Door for all time to come, or was liable to be closed at a certain stage. The Scholars of the later generation which produced no outstanding figure comparable to the towering genius of the first three Centuries, held that Ijtihad was a kind of self-curtailing process, no more needed with the passage of time. They held that the structure of Shariah had become complete. Ijtihad therefore, had outlived its utility.

Gate Closed:

In addition to the view that all the lacunae in the body of Law and Jurisprudence had been filled by the process of Ijtihad, and that Ijtihad was no longer needed, there were the social and historical factors inducing retrograde attitude on thought and action of the people. The Abbaside Regime had attained glory and splendour in all fields, and material prosperity was enjoyed by the people at large. But there was marked deterioration in religious and moral spheres everywhere in the country. The Ulama of the Royal Court had become notorious for corruption, submissiveness and even weakening of Faith.

With the decline in morals of both the Ulama and the Ummah, the watchful section of the people began to feel that the safety of Islam lay in rigidly pinning down all the Islamic thought and practice as they existed then, and that time had come for restriction of the powers of interference with the Shariah and of the process of interpretation. Under the circumstances, an Ijma of the Sunni Juristic Schools was convened, which took a unanimous decision that Ijtihad was no longer open for exercise. This decision of the undated Ijma-e Ummah was implemented by a *Fatwa* on the closure of *'Bab-al Ijtihad'*. The Gate of Ijtihad was thus closed for good in the World of Sunni Muslims.

Reasons for Closure:

Several reasons have been affirmed or surmised why the Gate of Ijtihad was closed. A few of them are mentioned below:

(A) By the end of the 3rd Century Hijri, the four great Imams had risen so high above all others, that a sense of frustration overtook the Jurists of the later generation. The idea grew that no one was entitled to exercise his own Judgment independently of the great Imams. The consequence of such impression was seen in the limitation of the function of Ijtihad. It was acknowledged that the right to formulate principles of Ijtihad was the privilege of only the Scholars of earlier Centuries.

(B) Some Scholars held that Ijtihad was a kind of self-curtailing process, less and less needed with the passage of time, as the feature of silence or of missing links in the Islamic Laws was steadily provided by its exercise. They forcefully argued that Ijtihad, having fulfilled its full-scale objective by their time, enabled Ijma to complete the body of Law, and was therefore no longer required to operate.

(C) Some pious men began to realise that philosophical thought alien to the spirit of Islam had been infiltrating into Islamic system of Religious outlook and social behaviour. This could be counteracted, as they felt, by banning all forms of innovations permeating through Ijtihad.

(D) A noted Western Scholar on Islamic History and Culture, W. Montgomery Watt has given yet another reason based on his studies. He writes, "Since it is not clear how the 'Gate'came to be closed, it would be worth trying to discover whether part of the motive for declaring the Gate closed was the desire to reduce Governmental pressure on individuals. A man is better able to resist pressure to accommodate his decision to reasons of State, if he is able to say, "I have no competence to vary such and such a decision". (R-1)

Stagnation in Community Life:

The telling effect of closure of the Gate was that nobody could thereafter be considered qualified for exercise of independent reasoning relating to any subject matter of Shariah. Even the discretion of making fresh interpretation of a matter already settled, was not available. There could be no Mujtahids any longer, but only Muqallideen who were entitled to follow Mujtahids of earlier times without insisting on any justification in support of their decrees. These Muqallideen might only quote Fatwas in conformity with earlier authorities, if there were differing opinions of earlier Jurists, the Muqallideen was at liberty to choose any one of them, without questioning the correctness of such Ruling. He could not go any further.

The immediate consequence of the ban imposed on Ijtihad was seen in the deprecation of individual thought and in the denial of exercise of one's own reason and Judgment. This was not in keeping with the spirit of the Holy Qur'an which has emphasised and reiterated the need to rely upon reason and understanding. With these intellectual impediments created as a result of closure of Ijtihad, the future of Muslims suffered heavily. The urge for acquisition of growing Knowledge gave place to mere imitation of past performance. Progress and advancement came to a standstill. Stagnation and inaction ruled supreme over the Community-life of Muslims.

Reaction of Intellectuals:

The thoughtful among the Muslims are confronted

with the question: Have the Muslims as a result of closure of Ijtihad, continued to progress as they did during the Ijtihad Era of 300 years from the 7th to the 9th Centuries, or have they gone down the ladder of material and spiritual advancement during the long span of a thousand years from the 10th to the 20th Centuries? The answer is obvious and well admitted on all hands. The Muslims have slided down deplorably in all spares of life due to loss of political power, lack of Education, growing poverty, sectarianism in religion and a host of degrading Economic, Social and Psychological factors.

No Wisdom in sealing the Door:

The older generation of Scholars who closed the Door of Ijtihad out-right, were in fact incapable of fore-sight as to how drastically God's World and the times and conditions of human life are going to change between the Medieval Age when they lived and the far distant Space Age, intervened by the Industrial, technological and electronic eras. They were incapable of imagination how their remote posterity and the ulterior species of Homo Sapiens are destined to proliferate in the over-populated Earth, and then to look for migration to other planets floating in Space of the limitless Universe.

These venerable good souls whose education and outlook were limited only to the extent of learning and vision available in the old world of a thousand years ago, and who, instead of following the Holy Qur'an's oft-repeated exhortations to rely upon one's own reasonings and exercise of Judgment, were irrationally driven to believe in a false dogma that the end of the World was near enough. With such mis-conceptions blurring their limited power of understanding, they took measures to halt the advance of human Civilization at the level of 4th Century Hijri (1000 AD) by closing all doors of progress and reformation, and to prohibit any further attempt to introduce new concepts intended to remodel the life and activity of the people.

Secondly, the learned Scholars were human beings after all, and were certainly subject to the minimum weakness of human behaviour. As such they were not expected to be completely free from an unconscious ego that they had reached the apex of human wisdom and that no individual after them was fit to claim elevation to a level of learning and knowledge equal to or higher than what they had attained. In their own way, they honestly felt that all doors of further legal expansion should be closed, so that no man of lesser attainment may induct corruption and evil. They were not prepared to admit that if the door was kept open, there was the possibility of men more talented than themselves coming in future and causing improvement over the legacy left by them. These were the unimaginative, if not self-conceited, Scholars who initiated or agreed to the sealing of the Door of Ijtihad once for all. This was not an act of wisdom or foresight.

Decree of Closure not Valid:

The holy Prophet had taken care personally in formulating and putting into operation the principle of Ijtihad. He did not give any indication that it may be terminated at any time in future. Neither did any of the Companions nor did the great Imams ever give an impression that Ijtihad is a temporary provision, liable to end after their life time or any future time. The Companions and the Imams also did not say that no one after them was authorised to operate Ijtihad. No books of Islamic Jurisprudence provide that nobody can operate Ijtihad after the life-time of the great Imams or other Mujaddids. No saint or savant was in a position to declare that no new circumstances would arise in the World after the 4th or the 6th Century Hijri.

So one may pertinently ask, how could the process of Ijtihad so wisely heralded by the Holy Qur'an and initiated by wisdom of the Prophet for providing adjustments against unexpected changes in future be terminated by a body of non-Prophets when more and more changes are sure to come as time marches on to Eternity? The Holy Qur'an does not support the closure. The Prophet did not authorise anybody to close the Door. The Decree of closure announced by any authority other than the Holy Qur'an and the Prophet can not be accepted as valid.

Moreover, there is an incontrovertible and firm ground to hold that the act of closure was strictly invalid. Ijma, the third source of Islamic Law ranking below the Qur'an and Sunnah, suffers from some basic limitations, namely, (i) Ijma can not operate in fields where the Qur'an and Sunnah have made clear provisions, and(ii) Ijma can not challenge, change or cancel the Law laid down in the Qur'an and Sunnah.

It is relevant to bear in mind that the process of Ijtihad has its firm root in verses of the Qur'an and precepts of the Sunnah. As such, no Ijma can have any authority to cancel, abrogate or halt the process of Ijtihad. The reported closure of Ijtihad by decision of an Ijma-e Ummat held in the 4th Century Hijri or thereafter, being outside its legal jurisdiction, is clearly invalid.

A Hoax by Frustrated Ulama:

Considering the ruinous effects of the closure of Ijtihad, it is pertinent to enquire if the group of Scholars declaring the ban were men of sufficient piety, learning and wisdom, so as to be considered worthy of taking drastic action in a matter which the great Imams and other notable Theologians of the 2nd and 3rd Centuries Hijri did not venture to think.

The momentous event took place some time during the period of Decadence of the early Medieval Age. It was at this time that feigned show of religiosity was eating into the body politic of Islam like Cancer. Religion was beginning to go astray towards the path of heresy. The still lingering influence of Hellenistic thoughts, the solemn Sufistic disciplines of Iranian origin, the Rationalistic Movement of Umayyad Era, the widespread materialism of Abbaside Regime and a host of such other historical, geographical and sociological bearings had contributed to the mental make up of the Ulama of the 4th Century Hijri and thereafter. Above all, the enormous distinction attained by the Imams and divines of the 2nd and 3rd Centuries Hijri was so high that no Scholar thereafter could ever hope to reach that height or outshine the talent of earlier generation of Scholars. A deep sense of frustration stole over the later Ulama, who naturally became demoralised and disconcerted.

It was again at this time that there was marked deterioration in talent and piety in the Muslim milieu. Intellectually and spiritually, it was an Era of mediocrity when there was no person of such talent and virtues as to be considered qualified to cancel or halt the process initiated by the Prophet himself. The holy Prophet said, "The best of the generations is my generation, then the second and then the third. Then will come a people in whom there is no good". Learned interpreters say that the Prophet meant a span covering a Century by his word 'generation'. So the prediction of the holy Prophet means that after the end of the first three Centuries, there will be decline in the quality of Muslim leaders. The last of the four great Imams died by the middle of 3rd Century. Thereafter the Scholars of the 4th Century Hijri may be deemed to be men. "in whom there is no good" in the words of the holy Prophet.

In order to weigh the wisdom and piety of the leaders who passed the Decree of Closure, the present Author issued a set of questionnaire to a number of prominent Theologians of India, with request to find out facts and furnish a comprehensive reply to the following questions, namely:

(i) In which year and in what place the Ijma which took the decision to terminate the process of Ijtihad was held?

(ii) What are the names, status and qualification of the leading Ulama involved in the decision?

The Theologians contacted were mostly top-ranking persons or institutions, namely, Maulana Syed Abdul Hafiz Salfi of Darbhanga, Dar-ul Ifta of Deoband, Mufti Azam of Saharanpur, Maktaba Faiz Ashraf of Jalalabad, Dar-ul Uloom of Bareli, Maulana Abu Mahfuz al-Karim Masoomi of Madrasah Alia, Calcutta, Maulana Dr. Abdur Rashid Qasmi of Deoband, Maulana Mohammad Aman-ullah of Senior Madrasah, Binjharpur and a few others.

Replies were received from three Referees, one of whom expressed inability to furnish the required information as no materials were available in spite of all possible efforts. The second Referee, Dar-ul Ifta of Dar-ul Uloom, Deoband, is one of the most prestigious and eminent Centers of Islamic Education in India. It furnished an elaborate reply in its Letter of Authority (Fatwa) No. 385/Jeem dated 1.4.1411 Hijri corresponding to 21.10.1990, signed by one Mufti and attested as correct by two other Muftis, and impressed with the official seal of the Institution, a copy of which may be seen at Appendix-B.

The third Theologian who responded is Maulana

Mufti Mahmoodul Hasan, Mufti Azam, Saharanpur, who was perhaps unable himself to find out the appropriate reply to the two questions sent to him, but took the trouble to forward the queries to Dar-ul Ifta, Deoband. The latter furnished a reply under the Official Seal and signatures of three Muftis, similar to the one sent originally by Dar-ul Ifta, Deoband, as at Appendix-B. This Appendix-B may be considered as the views of the Deoband and the Saharanpur Madrasahs of Theology. A summary of the letter is given below:

(i) "Hazrat Shah Waliullah (R.A.) in his book *'Al-Insaaf'* mentions that the obligations of Mujtahids is a secret *(Raaz)*, arising out of the *Ilham* (divine enlightenment) instilled into the hearts of Ulama-e Huq."

(ii) " After the 2nd Century Hijri, some Ulama-e Huq were enlightened by an *Ilham* from Al'ah Tabarak, which was regarded as *'Ijma-e Amali'* as distinguished from *'Ijma-e Qawli'*, the former being superior to the latter.

(iii) *"Ijma-e Amali* is one of Allah's secrets. All the Ulam-e Haq are bound by Faith to it on the principle of *Taqlid*. The two questions referred to by the present Author are not answerable, as they fall under the purview of *Ijma-e Amali,* which is based on a secret *Ilham* from Allah, not permissible to be disclosed to any private individual."

(iv) "Hazrat Shah Waliullah mentions in his book that in Hindustan, wherever there may be no Ulama of Maliki, Shafe'i or Hanbali Sects, the *Ilhams* of Allah are binding as *'Taqlid Wajib'* on all Hanafi Ulama, according to Imam Abu Hanifa. This is supported by a number of Hadith of the holy Prophet."

In order to assess the value of the above letter, it may be necessary to recall the two Questions sent to Dar-ul

Ifta, Deoband, with request to offer clear answer. The questions related to:

(a) The venue and year of decision of closure of Ijtihad;

(b) The names of Ulama heading the Decision-making authority.

None of the two questions has been answered. On the other hand, the enquirer is told that he is not entitled to acquire knowledge of the message based on divine *Ilham,* which is meant for enlightenment of only the Ulama-e Huq. So the Ummah must remain in dark, and must believe that they are unworthy of learning about the message of Allah by virtue of a Ruling which is declared as *Taqlid Wajib* for the Hanafi sect only. It is funny that the adherents of Maliki, Shafe'i, Hanbali *Aquidah* (creed) are free to accept or reject this imposition upon their religious faith, but the men belonging to Hanafi ideology must blindly follow the dogma without any dependence upon their reason or judgment. The whole plea may be dismissed outright, because it is against the spirit of the Holy Qur'an, which repeatedly asks Believers to make use of their reason and judgment in affairs of this World and the hereafter.

Moreover, the Deoband letter leads to further confusion and contradictions, as mentioned below:

(a) The letter implies that the decision of closure was taken "after the 2nd Century Hijri." But all other available accounts surmise the date to be after the 4th Century. On account of such difference with the general trend widely varying to the extent of 200 years, the date as mentioned by Deoband without giving any historical justification, seems to be mere guess work, and is unreliable and unacceptable.

(b) The decision of closure was based, not on Ijma-e Ummat but on an *Ilham* received direct from Allah. This is contrary to all other information on the subject, which generally affirm Ijma-e Ummat being the basis. This is the first time that an attempt has been made to tie the theory of *Ilham* to the termination of the process of Ijtihad. A dubious effort has been made by equating the *Ilham* from Allah with a novel concept of *Ijma-e Amali* of Ulama, and imposing the stamp of *'Taqlid Wajib'* upon such *Ijma-e Amali,* finally requiring the Hanafi Ulama to acquiesce in it as a Wajib obligation, even if the Ulama of all other sects, Maliki, Shafe'i and Hanbali do not agree to it.

(c) The alleged *Ilham* descended, not on any of the two great Imams, namely, Imam Shafe'i (died 204 AH) and Imam Hanbal (died 241 AH), who were alive after the 2nd Century Hijri, or on any other well-Known saint or Sufi who were alive during that time, but very curiously the *Ilham* alighted upon a number of such Ulama whose names, identity and purity of personal life can not be disclosed to any body. The year when the *Ilham* was enlightened in the hearts of the Ulama concerned, is also not to be disclosed.

(d) Ijma is an operation where a large number of participants are involved. Since the alleged *Ilham* has been classified as an Ijma, it means that the *Ilham* from Allah on this particular subject (closure of Ijtihad) was flashed upon the hearts of a large number of men. It is sacrilegious to think that Allah's *Ilham* is so cheap that one *Ilham* on one subject was sent simultaneously to say, 20, 30 or even 100 Ulama constituting the Ijma, and yet the names of these several so-called Ulama can not be divulged to the posterity.

(e) If it was the sacred intention of Allah Tabarak Ta'la to discontinue the process of Ijtihad by means of *Ilham,*

He could have chosen any of the Khulafa-e Rashideen or the great Imams for receiving the *Ilham*. Without any Divine intimation to stop the operation of Ijtihad, all the eminent personalities carried on the function as in the days of the Prophet. If the *Ilham had* terminated Ijtihad after the 2nd Century, the last two Imams would not have performed the operation at all. But they actually operated Ijtihad till they were alive. The alleged story of *Ilham* seems to have no reliable foundation. It appears to be a mere credulous, imaginary or visionary impression of some body, if not a hoax.

Lastly, there is a contradictory account of closure of the Gate of Ijtihad coming from a Turkish source. Sultan Abdul Hamid of Turkey was interested on the subject. One Turkish Scholar named Shaikh Hussain Afandi prepared and published a Journal, *"Hamidiya fi Haqiqat-ud diyanat-ul Islamia Wa Haqiqat-us Shariata Muhammadia,"* in which he mentioned that the Hanafi Ulama accepted the closure of *'Bab-al Ijtihad'* with effect from 328-29 Hijri. (R-2).

This scholar did not mention about any Ijma or *Ilham* being the source of the decision of closure, but wrote in a casual way that the Hanafi Ulama happened to believe in the closure of Ijtihad. There is no mention about the place where the decision was made. The names of Ulama who headed the decision-making body are not mentioned. This Turkish account does not find corroboration in any other report. There may be no justification in according historic authenticity to such an isolated and uncorroborated matter.

The Islamic Revolution is highly distinguished because all aspects of this mighty World-wide movement occurred in the full glare of history. The story of closure of Ijtihad is thoroughly anti-history, being based on guess work and on unconfirmed hearsay tales circulating in the Community's uncritical awareness from Century to Century. No serious student of Islamic History will lend credence to such ill-founded accounts.

The efforts to establish the identity of Authors of the Decree of Closure and also to locate the venue and the year of the significant event by reference to a number of prominent Theologians of India having failed, recourse was taken to consult the Works of eminent European Classical scholars considered well-versed in Islamic Culture and Civilization, or noted for intensive study, patient research work and comprehensive knowledge of Islamic subjects. One of them, W. Montgomery Watt, who delved deep in quest of the relevant historical truth, found nothing and mentioned politely, "It is not clear how the 'Gate' came to be closed." (R-1).

Failure of all these efforts may show, as one of the Theologians frankly admitted, that the plea of Ijma was the result of concoction by some less known and frustrated Ulama of no good name and fame, guided by jealousy and ulterior motive of preventing the possibility of other men earning credit by performance of fresh Ijtihad, which they themselves were unable to do. That is why no records are available regarding the time, place and leading brains behind the Closure.

The Theory of Closure on the basis of *Ilham* from Allah, may at best be a credulous and shallow imagination of an individual, unable to judge how the stoppage of Ijtihad might prove to be a disaster for the future of the Community.

The high importance of Ijtihad is obvious, because it was set in motion under the authority of the Holy Qur'an and implemented personally by the holy Prophet. The closure of Ijtihad is a matter of equal importance, for it was intended to put an end to the legal operation of a process approved by Allah and His Rasool. Yet the relevant details of closure are shrouded in a haze of obscurity resulting from cunning manoeuvres of evil minds and intellectual sterility of the times.

Dr. Iqbal, after critical studies, was satisfied that the story of closing the 'Gate' was a false propaganda carried out by "intellectually lazy" people, and finally concluded that the whole affair is a "pure fiction". The present study, after taking into account the theory of imaginative *Ilham*, and considering the conflicting and unconfirmed tales of Ijma-e Ummat, considers it reasonable to conclude that a band of self-seekig and frustrated Ulama played a hoax on the entire mass of innocent Muslims by circulating a concocted story of an Ijma deciding to close the Gate of Ijtihad for ever.

Protest and Reform:

The termination of the process of Ijtihad led to prolonged controversy. Many eminent thinkers sensed an impending disaster in the unfortunate decision. They were afraid that the banning of Ijtihad would have the effect of reducing the Laws of Islam to a state of immobility. Islam is a dynamic and mobile Religion, not stagnant or static in character. Any factor likely to make it stagnant is un-Islamic.

Learned men, possessing foresight of possible trend of future events are aware of the inevitability of impending changes which are likely to be drastic in character. They realise that the present and the future call for quick adaptation to changing conditions. Failure of the present and coming generations in making themselves adaptable will lead to collapse of the society in moral and material spheres.

At this exciting period of human History, some people may like to shut their eyes to the impending dangers of the fast changing World. Their attitude of always looking to the past prevents them from acquiring the ability to look to the future, and developing the necessary consciousness to plan the mode of survival through adaptation amidst changing circumstances. This is a fatal mistake, liable to demand a heavy price in life and prosperity of the erring generation.

Reformers--Hardliners and Progressive:

Under the circumstances, strong voice of protest against the decision to ban the process of Ijtihad began to be heard form time to time. Among the intellectuals offering protest, there are two categories. While both the categories, the Hardliners and the Progressive Thinkers, demanded revival of the process of Ijtihad, the former insisted on high and rigid qualification for persons authorised to operate Ijtihad. They lay down the highest level of Theological and Juristic qualification on all branches of the text and Commentaries of the Holy Qur'an, Hadith and all Schools of Jurisprudence, all cases of Ijma and Qiyas, together with the general knowledge of Worldly affairs. This yard-stick of qualification is so ideal that it is wellnigh impossible of realisation in a single individual. In fact, this sort of insisting on exceedingly high qualification is yet another way of keeping the Gate of Ijtihad closed.

The second category, the Progressive Thinkers, consider that persons with adequate insight into the provisions of the Qur'an and Hadith combined with good level of modern education, with a mind free from prejudice and character noted for honesty and integrity, are well-suited for exercising the powers of Ijtihad in the present times.

The older generation of conservative scholars, the Muqallid, who closed the Gate of Ijtihad outright, were rather frank and out-spoken, even though they happened to be uncompromising and non-forward looking austere disciplinarians. But the next generation of hard-core reformers, who believed themselves to be sensible modern Theologians, did the worse by condemning the old mentality of closing the Gate on the one hand, while on the other hand they prescribed the opening of the Gate by men so highly pious and learned that such persons were not actually to be found in a generation of population. In trying to correct the mis-conceptions of the old orthodox Muqallids, they themselves imposed unrealistic and utopian conditions on the qualification of Ijtihad Legist in such a manner as to render the whole process rigid enough for any practical application. They are in no way more desirable keeper of the community's conscience than the forbidding Muqallids.

The subject of appropriate qualification of Ijtihad Legists under the present day conditions has been considered in all aspects in Section IX ahead. The operation of Ijtihad should be carried out by persons considered well-qualified accordingly.

Reference

R-1 : *Islam and the Integration of Society* by W. Motgomery Watt, Routledge & Kegan Paul, London, 1961, page 243.

R-2 : *Al-Tauiyah* Monthly, Darya Ganj, New Delhi, for June, 1990, p.7 onwards.

Section VIII

PLEA FOR RE-OPENING

فَاعْتَبِرُوْا يَاُولِى الْاَبْصَارِ

So learn a Lesson, O ye who have eyes.
-Holy Qur'an: Al-Hashr (59:2)-

Views of Religious Leaders and Intellectuals:

Scholars of old Schools of Thought are generally satisfied about the termination of the process of Ijtihad some time between the 4th and the 6th Centuries Hijri. But other Scholars do not agree with this view on the basis of their knowledge of the historical and Theological aspects of Ijtihad. They hold such an opinion to be either unwise or unauthorised and empirical, and advocate their strong view to the contrary. Some of them assert that it was not a sound legal proposition to treat Ijtihad as closed, and that the Body which declared the closure had no tangible authority to take such a drastic action. They further urge that even if Ijtihad is deemed to have been closed rightly, the process must now be re-opened forthwith.

A brief outline of the thinking of some notable religious leaders and scholars on the continuation of the process of Ijtihad is given below. Sixteen prominent Thinkers are included in the review, namely:

Imam Abu Hamid Muhammad Al-Ghazali
Shaikh-ul Islam Hafiz Ibn Taimiyah
Shah Waliullah Mohaddis Dehlavi

Syed Jamaluddin Afghani
Mufti Muhammad Abduh of Egypt
Sir Syed Ahmad Khan
Maulana Abul Kalam Azad
Maulana Muhammad Ali of Lahore
Dr. Sir Muhammad Iqbal
Justice Syed Ameer Ali
Dr. K.G. Saiyidain
Maulana Sayyid Abul A'la Maududi
Maulana Abul Hasan Ali Nadwi
Maulana Taqi Amini of Aligarh
Maulana Muhammad Ismail of Gujranwala.
Hakeemul Ummat Maulana Ashraf Ali Thanavi (R.A.)

THE VIEWS

(1) Imam Abu Hamid Muhammad Al-Ghazali:

The spiritual eminence, intellectual zeal and powerful pen of Imam Ghazali (1058-1110 AD) enabled him to produce scores of authoritative literature in defence of Islam. He vigorously criticised the Theologians of his time, and deplored that Religious differences had become so widespread and acute that new sects were being formed on minor issues, while the system of Madrasah Education was decaying and public morals were declining. Mulana Abul A'la Maududi, in appreciation of the contribution of Imam Ghazali for revival of the moral, ethical and spiritual character of Islam, writes:

Imam Ghazali "revived the understanding of Islam, deplored blind faith, opposed rigid conformity and drew the people's attention towards the real source of guidance, viz. the Book of Allah and the Sunnah of His

Prophet. He revitalised the spirit of Ijtihad, and criticised all sects for their weakness and un-Islamic leanings, and urged them towards reform" (R-1).

(2) Shaikh-ul Islam Hafiz Ibn Taimiyah:

Hafiz Ibn Taimiyah (1263-1328 AD) was known for his unmatched erudition not attained by any Ulama of his time. He received "sound education in religious and secular Sciences. He had ardent desire for acquisition and comprehension of under-lying truths in Qur'anic Literature. So he studied about a hundred Commentaries of the Holy Scripture, including those of Hanbalite and Ash'arite Scholars. At the age of 23 years, he succeeded his father Shahabuddin Ibn Taimiyah as the Professor of Damascus University, a high post reserved only for the oldest and most eminent Theologian. His first lecture in the University created sensational reaction among the learned Divines of the City, who were overwhelmed with admiration and astonishment at the exceptional erudition of the young man." (R-2).

As a fearless social reformer, Ibn Taimiyah "not only raised a strong voice against rigid conformity (Taqlid), but successfully undertook Ijtihad also in the manner of the early religious doctors. He drew inspiration direct from the Book and the Sunnah and the lives of the Companions, studied the various Schools of Juristic thought with a critical mind, and deduced and established great many injunctions. Thus he was able to set open the Gate of Ijtihad, and demonstrated precisely how to use and exploit fully one's abilities in that field. Besides him, his great pupil Hafiz Ibn-e Qayyam concentrated his energies on unravelling the rationality behind Islamic Legislation, and produced unparalleled work on the Legislator's method and technique of Law-making in Islam. This unique work has been serving as a beacon of light for those who undertook Ijtihad in the past and will continue serving this great purpose in the future also. "(R-3).

(3) Shah Waliullah Mohaddis Dehlavi:

An acknowledged spiritual leader of Islam and celebrated Thinker of deep insight, sharp intellect and powerful pen, Shah Waliullah (1703-1763 AD) initiated a bold movement for eradication of social evils, and reconstruction of religious thought. He sought to interpret Islam on rational grounds in such a way as to bring it uptodate, so that it might adapt itself to the changing conditions of the modern World. As a prolific Author producing a wealth of authoritative Theological Works, he strongly advocated the necessity of taking resort to Ijtihad in almost all his writings. In the Preface to 'Musaffa', he writes:

"Ijtihad in every age is obligatory (on the Muslim Scholars). By 'Ijtihad' I mean the full understanding of the Shariah values (Ahkam) based on the fundamentals of Islam, the elucidation of their details and the compilation and codification of new Laws, although it may be in conformity with the approach adopted by the founder of a particular School."

The reason why I have spoken of Ijtihad as obligatory is that every age has its countless peculiar problems, and cognisance of the Divine Injunctions with regard to them is essential. The material which has already been written and compiled, it is not only insufficient but also embodies many differences of opinion. These differences can not be resolved without resort to the fundamentals of the Shariah, as also because the chain of authenticity leading back to the Mujtahids is probably disrupted.

Therefore the only way open is to review and reassess these differences against the principles of Ijtihad." (R-4).

(4) Syed Jamaluddin Afghani:

Syed Jamaluddin (1839-1897) was the Leader of Middle East Countries, where he initiated the two-pronged Reformation Movement of the 19th Century. The movement laid stress on the purification of Islamic Faith and Practice, as well as on unification of Muslim Nations into one single authority under the banner of Ottoman Caliphate. His untiring campaign throughout the Middle East powerfully stirred Islamic fervour, promoted inspiration behind the concept of Pan-Islamism, and contributed to the political uprising in Egypt and Persia. He vigorously exhorted Muslims to develop reason, discard rigid dogmas, and take to the study of Science. Prof. M. Jamil Hanafi says:

Jamaluddin "called for a reformed Islam, an Islam that would not continue to provide legitimacy for the debilitating political and economic patterns of Islamic Traditionalism. He advocated the re-opening of the gates of interpretation of Islamic Dogma." (R-5). In other words, Jamaluddin Afghani strongly advocated the re-opening of the Gate of Ijtihad.

(5) Mufti Muhammad Abduh of Egypt:

Mufti Abduh (1849-1905) was a young teacher in Al-Azhar University, and sincere enlightened modernist. He introduced a broader and a more Scientific concept of religious education. When he began to face opposition from conservative elements, he met their charge by expounding his thoughts in the form of a Commentary of the Qur'an which he wrote. He also formed a new Religious party named 'Salafiya', which was left to his disciple Shaikh Rashid Rida of Syria (1865-1935) to develop and disseminate.

"The Salafiyas uphold the traditions of early Muslim

leaders, and reject the authority of the Medieval Ulama. They regard themselves as 'Neo-Hanbalites', and hold that the Gate of Ijtihad is open, and that the individual has the right of interpretation of Islamic Theology and Law." (R-6)

(6) Sir Syed Ahmad Khan:

Syed Ahmad Khan (1817-1898) was a rationalist and modernist. Any principle or tenet of Islam that did not appear consistent with reason, was interpreted by him on rational basis. According to him, compatibility between acts and words of God is a fact, and can therefore be rationally proved to be a fact. His controversies over some orthodox views of the Ulama were centered round the theory that Islam does not teach anything which conflicts with reason. He laid unlimited emphasis on taking resort to Ijtihad, which is the inalienable right of every individual Muslim.

The Journal *'Tahzib-e Akhlaq'* edited by Sir Syed appeared in 1870. It raised a storm of protest when he tried to awaken Muslims by his bold advocacy of socio-religious reforms. In order to disseminate his revolutionary and many-sided new thinking, he wrote:

"Contemporary Muslims are entitled to practise Ijtihad or independent judgment on modern questions not covered by the Qur'an and some authentic Hadith." (R-7).

(7) Maulana Abul Kalam Azad:

Maulana Azad (1888-1958) has left an indelible mark in contemporary history as a distinguished scholar, veteran statesman and eminent Theologian. Apart from his lofty ideals pertaining to national integrity, educational progress and cultural advancement of the country, he maintained an unprejudiced mind and clear conscience with regard to precepts and practice of religion. He fearlessly attacked religious superstition and irrational rituals, and strongly advocated reformation of Islamic Faith on Qur'anic principles. He observed:

"I do not know what is Sunnism, and what the Shi'as believe in. I have full faith in Allah and His Book, and I acclaim the Prophet. I have also been bestowed with reason, and I go after established facts. What is white, remains white. What is black, remains black." (R-8).

The above words of the Maulana amount to clear reiteration of the principle of Ijtihad. He affirms his Faith first on Allah and on Qur'an, second on Prophet, and the last on his own reason and judgement. This is exactly the reply that Mu'az gave to the holy Prophet on the eve of his appointment as the Governor of Yemen. The Prophet heartily approved the reply.

Maulana Azad considered Ijtihad indispensable for enabling Muslim Society to keep pace with the march of time.

(8) Mulana Muhammad Ali of Lahore:

Mulana Muhammad Ali is an illustrious writer on Islamic literature, and is well-known for his English Translation of the Holy Qur'an. Another illuminating book coming from his pen is *'The Religion of Islam'*, wherein he has written a learned chapter on Ijtihad. He says:

"Reasoning or the exercise of Judgment in theological as well as legal matters, plays a very important part in the Religion of Islam, and the value of reason is expressly recognised in the Holy Qur'an. * * Ijtihad or the exercise of Judgment is expressly recognised in Hadith as the means by which a decision may be arrived at, when there is no direction in the Holy Qur'an or Hadith."

The Maulana concludes by observing as follows: "The impression prevailing in the Muslim World at present that no one has the right, even in the light of the new circumstances which a thousand years of the World's progress have brought about, to differ with the four Imams is entirely a mistaken idea. The right to differ with the highest of men below the Prophet is a Muslim's birth right, and to take away that birth right is to stifle the very existence of Islam. Under the present circumstances, when conditions have quite changed and the World has been moving on for a thousand years, while the Muslims have more or less stagnated, it is the duty of Muslim states and Muslim Peoples to apply their own Judgment to the changed conditions, and find out the ways and means for their temporal salvation." (R-9).

(9) Dr. Sir Muhammad Iqbal:

Dr. Iqbal (1876-1938), with a firm faith on the dynamic character of Islam, is the most out-spoken and vociferous advocate of Ijtihad among all the erudite Scholars of the Medieval and Modern Ages. He was deeply impressed by the Qur'anic Verse wherein Allah addresses mankind--"*And* to *those who exert, We show our Path*" (29:69). He says that the teaching of the Qur'an that life is a process of progress in Creation necessitates that each generation, guided but unhampered by the work of its predecessors, should be permitted to solve its own problems.

In his learned book *'The Reconstruction of Religious Thought in Islam'*, Dr. Iqbal has elaborately dealt with the theological, historical and traditional background of the principle of Ijtihad, and has condemned the unwise act of closing the 'Gate'. He says, "The closing of the Gate of Ijtihad is pure fiction suggested partly by the crystallization of legal thought in Islam, and partly by that intellectual laziness which, especially in the period of spiritual decay, turns great Thinkers into Idols. If some of the later doctors have upheld this fiction, modern Islam is not bound by this voluntary surrender of intellectual independence." (R-10).

Dr. Iqbal was an admirer of the modern sociological concepts prevailing in Turkey, where the principle of Ijtihad was working in the religious and political thinking of the Nation. He was impressed with the religious reforms introduced by Said Halim Pasha, the Grand Vizier of Turkey, who held that the earliest ideals of Islam had been lost through the influence of local heritage, and that it was necessary to tear off from Islam the hard crust which had immobilised its dynamic outlook on life, and to replant the original verities of freedom, equality and reason. With this background, Iqbal strongly advocated the necessity of taking resort to Ijtihad with a view to rebuild the Laws of Shariah in the light of modern thought and expediency.

Dr. Iqbal deplored the tendency of false reverence for the past as manifested in the temperament of Legists and Jurists of the Medieval Age, and felt that such a tendency was contrary to the inner impulse of Islam. Iqbal agreed with eminent thinkers like Ibn Taimiyah, Ibn-i Hazm and many others who held that Ijtihad is a sound principle of Law, open for the Muslim community for all times.

(10) Justice Syed Ameer Ali:

Justice Syed Ameer Ali's advocacy of an individual's right of reason and judgement in Islamic Jurisprudence has been explicitly summarised by Mr. M. Hidayatullah, ex-Chief Justice of India as follows:

"Ameer Ali saw in Islam great promise of development, and held it to be in conformity with the progressive demands of humanity. He bewailed that the stagnation was principally due to the notion that the right to exercise of private judgment ceased with the early Legists, that its exercise in modern times was sinful, and that a Muslim in order to be regarded as an orthodox follower of Muhammad should belong to one or other of the schools established by the schoolmen of Islam, and abandon his judgment absolutely to the interpretations of men who lived in the 9th Century, and could have no conception of the necessities of the 20th. He advised breaking these shackles and trusting to reason." (R-11).

Justice Ameer Ali was candid and potent supporter of validity of Ijtihad at all times, and was critical of the attitude of conservative Thinkers guided by erroneous notions of closure of the Gate.

(11) Dr. K. G. Saiyidain:

Dr. Saiyidain was the Education Secretary of India and he served as the visiting Professor to Columbia University, Winsconsin University and Standford University, and was the World President of the New Education Fellowship. He went to Sudan and Iraq as the Head of Education Commission.

Dr. Saiyidain writes: "Many religious persons have been misled into adopting the view that there is no scope for exercise of mind in the field of religion, that everything is given ready-made in the Scriptures, that the duty of all subsequent Commentators and students is to accept whatever has been said by earlier writers unquestioningly, and not to try and plumb the depths of meanings in a critical spirit."

"Many of the Theologians closed the Door of Ijtihad- the right of the thoughtful individual to exercise his personal thinking and judgment on matters about which he may not be satisfied with the opinion expressed by earlier interpreters and commentators. In fact, it is easier today to exercise Ijtihad, because all the facilities of knowledge and research which have become available to us since. It is all the more necessary to do so because great monumental changes in human life and problems have occurred in the meanwhile." (R-12).

(12) Maulana Syyid Abul A'la Maududi:

Maulana Maududi (1903-1979) was a valiant fighter of the 20th Century for the revival and restoration of Islamic Faith in its original pure form. He wrote a large number of books for religious awakening of the Muslims and for reconstruction of religious thought according to the earliest tenets of Islam. *'Tafheem-ul Qur'an,* the famous commentary of the Holy Qur'an in six volumes is one of the important products of his vast learning, deep insight and versatile pen.

The Maulana bewailed at the failure of great Mujahideen of the 18th and 19th Centuries in achieving results in spite of life-long struggle and earnest efforts. In his book *'Tajdid-o Ihya-i-Deen',* he elaborately examines the question that comes to his mind, namely, 'How could the British build a vast prosperous Empire in India, thousands of miles away from their home, while the Indian Mujahideen engaged in life-long struggle failed to establish an Islamic State in their homeland? The elaborate study concludes with two findings relating to the failure of Islamic Movement in its conflict with the Western materialist polity, as given below:

First finding: Although the revival of religious education and practice of Shariah are essential for the renaissance of Islam, yet this is not enough and something more is required for achieving final success. Matters needed in addition to the above are the full support and backing of modern science, constructive thought, competence in Arts and Technical skill, which have jointly combined to make the Western Nations stronger than the Muslim peoples.

Second finding: It is quoted verbatim as follows: "The work of revival and reconstruction in modern times demands a new Power for Ijtihad. The insight and power of interpretation displayed by Shah Waliullah and earlier Mujtahids and Mujaddids can not cope with the present day situations. The new Age accompanied by new means and powers has brought with it new evils and produced countless new problems of life, which could not even have crossed the mind of the Shah Saheb and the early Doctors. These conditions were only known to Allah who imparted these to His Messenger through His Grace. Therefore, the only source of guidance and inspiration for an ideological Movement for the renaissance of Islam in this Age are the Book of Allah and the Sunnah of His Prophet. Then in the light of this guidance, such an independent power of IJTIHAD is needed as may carve out a highway for action." (R-13).

Maulana Maududi, the greatest spiritual leader of the 20th Century, who is held in high esteem and reverence by lakhs of admirers and devotees in India and Pakistan, has made an intellectual survey of the politico-religious affairs of the present day Muslims of the sub-continent, as mentioned above, and has come to the most sensible conclusion that three vital conditions must be attained by the Muslim society, if it is to stand shoulder to shoulder with other advanced nations of the World, namely:

(i) Religious education with practice of Shariah;

(ii) Education in Western Science and Arts;

(iii) Opening the Gate of Ijtihad.

Lastly, it is worth serious attention that the Maulana is emphatic that religious education and practice of Shariah though essentially necessary, are not enough in the present Age which "has brought with it new evils and produced countless new problems of life." The progress of Islamic Culture and Civilization was stopped when the Gate of Ijtihad was closed. The Muslim community can not achieve progress unless the Gate is opened.

(13) Maulana Abul Hasan Ali Nadvi:

Maulana Abul Hasan Ali Nadvi is the Rector of Dar-ul Uloom, Nadwatul Ulama, India, and Member of the Standing Committee of the World Muslim Organisation (*Rabita-e Alam-e Islam*), Saudi Arabia, Member of the Advisory Committee of the University of Medina and of the Academy of Arts and Letters of Damascus. He has written about 50 books in Arabic and Urdu, many of which have been translated into English, French, Turkish and other Languages. In his book *'Islam and the World'*, the Maulana writes about Jihad and Ijtihad as follows:

There being no separate realms of God and Caesar in Islam, the Muslim Caliphate or Imamat calls for a large variety of human qualities. A Caliph or Imam should be, in addition to possessing a high degree of personal virtues, keenly alive to the needs of Jihad and ijtihad. Jihad is an Islamic terminology meaning to strive to One's utmost for what is noblest object on Earth. Ijtihad means the ability to cope with the ever-changing pattern of life's requirements. It calls for a deep insight into the soul of Islam, and a thorough knowledge of the basic principles of Islamic Jurisprudence."

"The whole course of Islamic History is lighted up with the crusading endeavours of conscious, determined, brave-hearted men who, like the true Successors of the Prophet, faced the challenge of the time and restored, revived and kept on moving the Millat by resorting to Jihad and Ijtihad. These two principles which embody the dynamism of Islam, could never suffer a vacuum in its structure. They remained operative ceaselessly in the body of Islam as living factors, holding aloft the Torch of Religious endeavours in the midst of severest tempests." (R-14)

(14) Maulana Taqi Amini:

Maulana Taqi Amini, Dean of the Faculty of Theology, Aligarh Muslim University, is the Author of several books on Islamic Law. He strongly advocates that there is no substance in the claim that the Gate of Ijtihad is closed. He holds that Ijtihad provides a dynamic and progressive character to Islamic Jurisprudence, and he categorically asserts that there is no bar to exercise free Judgment in the form of Ijtihad in justifiable cases at the present time. Reconstruction of Islamic Laws, which has become necessary due to changed conditions now, needs sincere efforts through wise and judicious interpretative operation, and so Ijtihad is imperative under the contemporary conditions.

The Maulana says, "interpretation is not only permitted but required by the true nature of Islamic Instruction. Believers are enjoined not only by express instruction to undertake the function of an interpreter and Law-giver, but implied also." (R-15)

(15) Maulana Muhammad Ismail of Gujranwala:

Maulana Muhammad Ismail of Punjab is an eminent Theologian of Salfi School of Reformers. His writings and discourses are highly valued in the field of Islamic Jurisprudence and Social History. He writes that the purity of Islamic tenets were maintained by the guidance received from Sahaba, Tabe'in, Imams and Ulama from the 1st to the 3rd Century Hijri. Thereafter sectarian feelings arose and the people began to get themselves attached to one particular Imam and to disregard the other three.

Under the circumstances, the creed of *'Taqlid'* or unthoughtful allegiance to particular Dogma began to spread among the masses since the 4th Century Hijri. Thereafter the Ulama relied upon the Rulings of Hedaya or Shami or some such authority of the Hanafi School, and issued Fatwas feeling satisfied that they had correctly shown the path of Shariah to the enquirer. They would not bother to draw authority from the Holy Qur'an or Hadith. Similar was the way of the Ulama of Shafe'i, Maliki and Hanbali Schools of Thought.

Freedom of thought was thus tabooed. Whenever a social or legal problem arose, decision had to be taken on the basis of precedents. Independent exercise of Judgment and fresh examination of propositions were forbidden. This process gave rise to the termination of the rights and privileges under the principle of Ijtihad. The Gate of Ijtihad was closed for good.

The Maulana observes that under the atmosphere of misguided Faith and unholy practices as prevailing in the 4th Century Hijri, the process of Ijtihad was terminated. The Hanafi Ulama agreed to this decision. An appearance was kept up as if there was the Divine approval behind the decision, but in fact there was no mention anywhere in the Holy Qur'an or Hadith about the closure of the process any time in human history. The Maulana emphasises that the closure of Ijtihad was the malafide handiwork of unimaginative and indolent persons. (R-16)

(16) Hakeemul Ummat Maulana Ashraf Ali Thanavi (R.A.)

The Maulana, who is the renowned Author of 'Behishti Zewar' and of a series of religious and popular books, writes that 'Ijtihad-e Mutlaq' (Ijtihad formulated on basic principles) remains closed from the 4th Century Hijri, but in respect of issues which did not exist during the time of early Authorities, and on which the early Authorities did not offer specific rulings, the exercise of Ijtihad remains open as before. He further clarifies that in every age, men capable of exercising Ijtihad are available, for otherwise the Shariah Law will not be complete and useful. The Maulana concludes by observing that Ijtihad as mentioned above remains operative now as well as for ever till the Day of Qiyamat. (R-17)

Reference

R-1 : *A Short History of the Revivalist Movement in Islam* by Syyid Abul A'la Maududi, Markazi Maktaba Islamia, Delhi, 1973, p.54.

R-2 : *Ulama* by Moinuddin Ahmed, Kitab Bhavan, New Delhi, 1990, p.40.

R-3 : *A Short History* vide R-1 above, p.60.

R-4 : *A Short History* vide R-1 above, p.84.

R-5 : *Islam and the Transformation of Culture* by M. Jamil Hanifi, Asia Publishing House, 1974, p.38.

R-6 : *Ulama* vide R-2 above, p.48.

R-7 : *Eight Lives* by Raj Mohan Gandhi, Roli Books

International, 1986, p.31.

R-8 : *Abul Kalam Azad* by Arsh Malsiani, Publications Division, New Delhi, 1976, p.104.

R-9 : *The Religion of Islam* by Maulana Muhammad Ali, S. Chand & Co. New Delhi, p.115.

R-10: *The Reconstruction of Religious Thought in Islam* by Dr. Sir Muhammad Iqbal, Kitab Publishing House, Delhi, 1974, p.178.

R-11: *Mulla's Principles of Mahomedan Law*, 18th Edition, N. M. Tripathi (P) Ltd. Bombay, 1977, p.xxx.

R-12: *Islam, the Religion of Peace* by Dr. K. G. Saiyidain, Jamia Nagar, New Delhi, 1976, p.179-80.

R-13: *A Short History* vide R-1 above, p.99.

R-14: *Islam and the World* by Abul Hasan Ali Nadwi, Academy of Islamic Research, Lucknow, 1973, p.91.

R-15: *Fundamentals of Ijtihad* by Maulana Taqi Amini, Idarah-e Adabiyat-e Dilli, Delhi, 1986, p.3.

R-16: *Al-Tauiyah* Monthly, Daryaganj, New Delhi, for June, 1990, p.7 onwards.

R-17: *Ijtihad-o Taqlid ka Akhiri Faisalah* by Mohd. Zaid Mozaheri Nadvi, Bandah, U.P., pp. 15-16.

Section IX

QUALIFICATION OF IJTIHAD LEGIST

A person entitled to formulate and pronounce Ijtihad is called a Mujtahid (Ijtihad Legist). There are different views with regard to the qualification of a Mujtahid, which may be classified under three standards, as mentioned below:

(A) Orthodox Standard:

According to the orthodox view, the qualification of a Mujtahid is highly rigid, and is centered round the full-scale knowledge of comprehensive Islamic Theology and Jurisprudence, namely:

(i) Comprehensive knowledge of the Qur'an in all branches of its grammar, commentaries and interpretations;

(ii) Knowledge of Sunnah with its lines of transmission, texts and varieties of significance;

(iii) Knowledge of Qiyas in all its aspects.

These are all-round high attainments, perhaps too high to expect in an individual of the present generation. Maulana Taqi Amini, a noted enthusiastic Scholar supporting the opening of the Gate of Ijtiahd says, "An expert interpreter is that Scholar who analyses the legal precepts and investigates the realities implicit therein, and explains the difficult points involved. A Jurist who possesses the technical skill required for interpretation could only be designated as an expert Interpreter, and no other Scholar, wise man or Edict-writer can usurp this function according to the principles of Islamic Jurisprudence." (R-1)

After setting the above high standard of Theological qualification of Ijtihad Legists, the Maulana pessimistically deplores, "Unfortunately, that level of intellect and wisdom has not been achieved which promotes and develops interpretative effort and enquiry in the field of law." Prescribing a set of qualification which is obviously too high, and then lamenting over no body being able to achieve it, virtually amounts to keeping the Gate of Ijtihad shut as before. Thus the Orthodox standard of qualification seems to be quite difficult to acquire in the present time.

Moreover, scholars with Orthodox Standard of Education have no Scientific background, which attainment is highly commended in *Surah Al-e Imran.* True reverence for God and His worship, coupled with scientific knowledge is a mark of wisdom and understanding, and both these attainments are necessary for a man considered fit to lead the community in religion and worldly affairs. Orthodox type of education does not make a man fit for such a double role.

(B) Progressive Muslims' Standard:

The ideas with regard to the qualification of an Ijtihad Legist, as advocated by progressive intellectuals vary widely from absolute freedom in exercise of Judgment by every individual Muslim to the cautious operation of Ijtihad only by well-educated men of honesty and integrity. It is not considered necessary to elaborate the views of those who advocate unrestricted freedom in the operation of Ijtihad by each and every Muslim, for the simple reason that such a liberty may degenerate into licence, and the person claiming the right to operate Ijtihad may consciously or unconsciously cross the line of validity, and regretably get into an arena considered un-Islamic by the yardstick of the Qur'an and Hadith.

The views of the other Section among Progressive Muslims who plead for exercise of the function by men of Knowledge, honesty and integrity, deserves consideration. The views of two typical advocates of such thinking are mentioned below:

(i) Maulana Muhammad Ali of Lahore, translator and commentator of the Holy Qur'an holds that under the present conditions, when the World has gone far ahead of the olden days of the holy Prophet, and when the Muslims are stagnating in all walks of life unlike what they were during the early Islamic Era, it would not be desirable to insist on rigid and abstruse proficiency in Islamic Religious Scriptures alone as adequate qualification for an Ijtihad Scholar. He further says, "The impression prevailing in the Muslim World at present that no one has the right even in the light of the new circumstances which a thousand years of the World's progress have brought about, to differ with the four Imams, is entirely a mistaken one. The right to differ with the highest of men below the Prophet is a Muslim's birth-right, and to take away that birth-right is to stiffle the very existence of Islam. Under the present circumstances, when conditions have quite changed and the World has been moving on for a thousand years, while the Muslims have more or less stagnated, it is the duty of Muslim States and Muslim peoples to apply their own Judgment to the changed conditions, and find out the ways and means for their temporal salvation". (R-2).

(ii) Another Author of repute, Kemal A. Faruki of

Karachi, has voiced a strong plea for change in the qualification traditionally required in a Mujtahid. He advocates that status in community, reputation for integrity in economic pursuits and noteworthy success in life as a whole are better criteria than abstruse canonical learning in Theology and a meticulous knowledge of Arabic grammar and legal lore. He writes, "I believe that considerably more is required than being an Alim, when one uses the word 'Alim' in its literal sense of 'one possessing knowledge'. For a person to be worthy of being entrusted with the formulation of Ijtihad, it is necessary that besides possessing knowledge, he should possess integrity of character as well, and these two qualities, integrity and knowledge, as we know to our cost, are not always found to co-exist, nor does one necessarily follow the other. To knowledge, then I would suggest that, integrity and honesty must be prefixed as essential preliminaries, and political conditions created which enable integrity and honesty to be assessed." (R-3)

Obviously, there is sense and convincing reason in holding that men with good modern education and conversant with current World trends must also possess spotless moral character, honesty and integrity in order to be fit for exercising the powers of Ijtihad. Good modern education and wide general Knowledge, first of all, are necessary because the early Islamic Era was very much different from the present times. Life was simple and slow then, now it is complex and fast-moving. Tardy camel caravans have given way to swift Air transport of today. Man was subservient to Nature then, now he has conquered it and has annihilated time and space. Knowledge, vision and outlook were limited then, now they are boundless. In such an eventful period of incredible growth and drastic changes in all spheres of human affairs, particularly in the context of vast expansion in the horizon of learning, the qualification of an eligible Ijtihad Scholar must be considerably different from what it was a thousand years back. Any such Scholar equipped with the Medieval stock of knowledge will make a poor show in the diverse Scientific atmosphere of today.

Secondly, the insistence on the qualities of integrity and honesty in addition to good modern education is highly significant, as may be judged from a few historical instances given below. Maulana Abul Hasan Ali Nadwi, the reputed international Arabic scholar, has drawn a sensational picture of the wretched character of an eminent Alim with Medieval education. He writes, "One of the learned Scholars in Akbar's entourage was Mulla Abdullah Sultanpur. He was supposed to be the infallible Guide and Expositor of the Faith, and had been conferred the title of 'Makhdum-ul-Mulk'. He had given a *Fatwa* that the Ordinance of Pilgrimage to Mecca was no longer binding, perhaps for the reason that he might not himself be called upon to perform the pilgrimage. He had also invented a device for avoiding payment of the legal alms *(Zakat) due* upon his wealth. He had made such a pile of wealth during Akbar's time that several boxes filled with gold bricks were later unearthed from his ancestral cemetery where they had been buried under pretext of dead relations." (R-4)

A few other typical cases of heinous character of Scholars with Madrasah education are given in the present Author's book 'Ulama'. He writes, 'Maulana Meer Abdul Hai, the Chief Mufti of Akbar's Court, was not only an inveterate drunkard, but was also steeped in pomp and luxury. Qazi Abdul Wahab, the *Qazil Qazat* (Chief Justice) of Gujrat in Emperor Aurangzeb's reign, acquired so much of illegal wealth that the wealthy of his age became jealous of him. On one occasion, an amount of Rupees Three Lakhs belonging to him was looted on the highway. When he died, Rupees Eight Lakhs in Moghul coins were found in his personal treasury, which was distributed among his four sons." (R-5)

The above instances are only a few out of countless cases showing how high education and dignified status in life are not necessarily an index of virtuous character. One must not over-estimate these learned men, for there were many pseudo-Ulama among them who could in no way be considered as honest and virtuous, as they were adept at giving crafty advice to Rulers who sought to justify their reprehensible deeds. The views held by the modern Reformers and Theorists that the qualities of honesty and integrity must be added to high modern education in respect of Ijtihad Functionaries, are sound and sensible.

(C) The Qur'anic Standard:

The Qur'an is the holy Book of guidance for mankind. Its sacred Verses show the right Path, not only for spiritual enlightenment but also for worldly affairs on all occasions of peace or war time. *Surah An-Nisa* says:

وَإِذَا جَآءَهُمْ أَمْرٌ مِّنَ الْأَمْنِ أَوِ الْخَوْفِ أَذَاعُوا بِهِۦ ۖ وَلَوْ رَدُّوهُ إِلَى
الرَّسُولِ وَإِلَىٰٓ أُولِى الْأَمْرِ مِنْهُمْ لَعَلِمَهُ الَّذِينَ يَسْتَنۢبِطُونَهُۥ مِنْهُمْ

Meaning- *"And if any tidings, whether of safety or fear, come unto them they spread it around; whereas if they had referred it to the Messenger and to such of them as are in Authority, those among them who are able to think out the remedy, would have done the needful."*

-Holy Qur'an: *Surah An-Nisa (4:83)*

There is clear indication that in times of safety or fear (Peace or War), the Muslims should not make unnecessary fuss about the situation, but should refer the matter to the Holy Prophet and to *Ulu'l-amr,* meaning men of Authority who are competent to take proper action. It is obvious that after the life-time of the holy Prophet Muslims should always seek the advice of eminent men of the society, styled as *Ulu'l-amr.* Such eminent men have been named in other Qur'anic Verses as *Ulu'l-albab* (3:190-91), meaning men of wisdom and understanding, and also as *'Alimeen'* (30:22), meaning men of learning. The term *'Alimeen'* is the plural of *'Alim'.*

According to the implications of the above Verses, the persons described as men of 'Amr', or of *'Albab'* or as *'Alimeen',* are the most eminent among all men of the society next only to the holy Prophet, and their advice should be sought on all occasions of peace or war. As the concept of Ijtihad was born out of Qur'anic Verses such as Verse 29:69 and Verse 4:83, it would be quite logical to entrust the operation of Ijtihad to the care of those persons who bave been commended in the Qur'an as men of wisdom, understanding, authority and learning. In other words, the exercise of Ijtihad can best be done by persons styled as Ulu'l-amr *Ulu'l-albab* and *Alims.*

It is now necessary to identify these three classes of men in the society. Such identification can be correctly done by considering the attributes described in the Text of the Qur'an about each category, as mentioned below:

(a) 'Ulu'l-amr are men of authority or command. The Ayat 4:83 clarifies the notion of these men as those who are able to think out and provide remedy in times of security as well as fear, meaning peace and war, and they are the next to the holy Prophet. This indicates the relevance of persons who are in charge of law and order of the Country. The fact that they have been mentioned as alternative to the holy Prophet shows that they must be men noted for good performance in religion. In other words, men of 'Amr' signifies God-fearing Rulers or Administrators.

(b) *'Ulu'l-albab'* are men possessing *'lub'*. Ayats 3:190-91 recounts the qualification of men of *Albab* by mentioning that such men have proper understanding of (i) creation of the Heavens and the Earth; (ii) the alteration of night and day; (iii) and that such men remember Allah standing, sitting or reclining. Therefore, the men of *Albab* are the men who practise remembrance of God with pursuit of science, combine spirituality with secular competence, and are noted for moral greatness and material advancement. In other words, men of *Albab* are Scientists with eminence in religious life and prosperity in worldly status.

(c) *'Alimeen'* is the same as Ulama, both the words being the plural of the term 'Alim' which is singular and means a learned man. Ayats 30:19 to 22 of Surah Ar-Rum recounts the qualifications of 'Alimeen' or the Ulama. According to the Qur'an, the Alimeen are persons who are capable of understanding and reflecting upon natural phenomena and Scientific principles as mentioned below:

The *Alimeen* or Ulama are persons capable of understanding:

(a) Ayat 30:19- How life came out of lifeless objects such as rocks, and how lifeless objects come out of living organisms; and also how the Earth can come into existence after its extinction;

(b) Ayat 30:20- How man is created out of dust;

(c) Ayat 30:21- How one sex is created for the comforts of the other sex;

(d) Ayat 30:22- How the Heavens and the Earth were created and how different languages and colour of men came into play.

The Holy Qur'an finally says that the above instances imply 'portents for men of knowledge', or tokens of understanding for those who are considered as *Alimeen* (Ulama). Therefore, persons who possess knowledge of Biology, Chemistry, Cosmology, Astronomy, Anthropology, Language Science and other relevant Sciences, are entitled to be called Ulama. There is no indication in the Holy Qur'an that persons ignorant of these sciences may be called Ulama.

Therefore, if the Qur'anic standard is to be adopted for the function of Ijtihad, the persons entitled to carry on the function should be:

either (i) an Administrator with good knowledge and practice of religion;

or (ii) a Scientist who is eminent in religious life and high in moral and material fields;

or (iii) an Alim who in addition to his proficiency in Arabic and Islamic learning, also holds qualification in one or more of the Secular Sciences named above.

Madrash Degree-holders not suitable as Ijtihad Legist:

The education given in Indian Madrasahs cover subjects pertaining to Theology and Jurisprudence, but not to secular Sciences. The Holy Qur'an speaks of Alims and men of wisdom who are good both in religious and secular learning. The products of Madrasah education are not blanced with knowledge of both the disciplines. Such men will not fit into the role of an Ijtihad functionary, because he must be a person with good religious background and secular education, both.

In this connection it may be relevant to mention that several eminent scholars of the Islamic World hold poor opinion of Madrasah educated men, or the Ulama of the Medieval and Modern Ages. One thousand years back, Imam Ghazali was unhappy to find the Ulama not fit to offer guidance to the Muslim community. In his book of undying fame, *'Ihya Uloom-id Din'*, he observed, "Ulama are the physicians, but these days they are themselves confined to sick-bed, and are unable to cure others." (R-6)

Imam Ghazali was the revered Mujaddid of his time, and is held in high esteem and respect at all times due to his erudition, piety and Islamic fervour. He must have found some cogent reasons for passing sweeping remarks that the Ulama are "responsible for the all round religious and moral degradation of the Muslim peoples." (R-7). The same kind of unfavourable opinion is also held by many other religious leaders like Hafiz Ibn Taimiyah, Shah Waliullah, Maulana Abul Kalam Azad and others. In the opinion of these Scholars, the Ulama are not capable of proving themselves useful to the Muslim community because they have fallen from the high Qur'anic standard of 'Men of Wisdom and Understanding'. The controversial type of sectarian education that they are receiving from later-day Madrasahs, and their love of power, money and leadership, which have developed in their character since the Mediveval times, are the main reasons why these Ulama have been deprived of the eminence and dignity associated with the Ulama of early Centuries of Islam.

Maulana Abul Kalam Azad in his learned discourses

titled *'Tazkirah'* has strongly condemned the conduct and activities of Ulama qualified with Madrasah education. He says, "The self-seeking disposition and lack of righteousness as seen among the Ulama, have proved to be the scourge for the community. The present day Ulama have discarded the observance of many of the humanitarian provisions declared compulsory in the Shariah. It may be possible for reptiles to live in a common habitat, but among the Ulama, one individual can not agree to live in peaceful co-existence with another. Like dogs, they fight with sharp claws and biting teeth whenever a bone is thrown at them." (R-8).

Among the learned men of the present Age, there are many who entertain similar sad opinion about the Ulama. Maulana Abul Hasan Ali Nadwi, an Arabic Scholar of international repute says, "In the 16th Century, the indolence of mind, slavish pedantry and blind imitation (among the Muslims) became complete. One does not find even one in a hundred among the Ulama of the last four Centuries who may with justice be called a genius, or who may have produced anything to set beside the bold and noble intellectual activities of the earlier Centuries." (R-9).

Another Scholar of modern times, Maulana Taqi Amini, Dean of the Faculty of Theology of Aligarh Muslim University, says that learned men entrusted with the interpretation of the Qur'an and Sunnah, are "not motivated by a sincere desire to find out solution for the many problems and issues faced by the Muslims. On the contrary, these exercises are undertaken to keep the leadership intact and to keep the scholarly flavour alive. In short, it is all done by way of amusement for personal aggrandisement, where objectivity and true scholarship are always a victim of vain discourses." (R-10)

A leading connoisseur of legal affairs and Authority

on Muslim Law, Dr. Tahir Mahmood, has given a historic account of the ineffective and useless role of Ulama in matters of Reform of Islamic Laws. His well-documented observations as furnished in his book *'Muslim Personal Law'* are extracted below:

"The Hanafi Ulama of India are broadly divided into two ideological sections, Deoband and Bareli. The two sections have enormous differences, and can not agree with each other's view point. Besides, there is a sizable group of Muslims who describe themselves as 'Ahl-e Hadith', and who agree neither fully with Deobandis nor entirely with Barelvis."

"It is naive to expect that Ulama of India, having such tremendous differences would unanimously agree even on a single item of Reform, if at all they agree to discuss it. It will be remembered that when Mustafa Kamal Pasha of Turkey set up in 1920 a Committee of the Ulama to consider Reform of Family Law in that Country, after being in session for so many years, the Committee failed to agree even on a single principle, and Mustafa Kamal had, in despair to adopt the ready-made Swiss Civil Code. In India, each group of Ulama (commanding innumerable followers) has its own interpretation of the Qur'an and Sunnah. They will take ages to express a unanimous opinion on any Reform to be applied to all Muslims alike. And even if they have agreed on any Reform, they will not like the State to take action."(R-11).

Apart from the highly unfavourable views of eminent Muslim Scholars who are not in favour of entrusting any sort of responsible or intellectual function to Ulama, it is shocking to note that the holy Prophet's Hadith records severe condemnation of the conduct and performance of the Ulama of later Age (meaning the present times). Mishkat-ul Masabih, the authentic collection of Hadith by

Shaikh Muhammad bin Abdullah Tabrizi, records the text of Hadith No. 276 (R-12) as follows:

عُلَمَآؤُهُمْ شَرٌّ مَنْ تَحْتَ اَدِيْمِ السَّمَآءِ مِنْ عِنْدِهِمْ
تَخْرُجُ الْفِتْنَةُ وَفِيْهِمْ تَعُوْدُ. ——— مشکوٰۃ، کتاب العلم

meaning, "These Ulama will be the worst people under the Heaven, and mischief will begin from them, and will revert to them."

The Hadith cited above is also mentioned in another Treatise 'Muqaddamah Dar Mustalahat-i hadith' by Shaikh Abdul Huq Mohaddis Dehlavi in Hadith No. 257 at page 76.

Again in another Sahih Hadith, the holy Prophet says:

تَكُوْنُ فِيْ اُمَّتِيْ فَزْعَةٌ فَيَصِيْرُ النَّاسُ اِلٰى عُلَمَآئِهِمْ
فَاِذَا هُمْ قِرَدَةٌ وَّخَنَازِيْرُ. ——— کنز العمال

meaning, "A period of anxiety and confusion will come upon my Ummat, when they will approach the Ulama for guidance, but they will find the Ulama in the likeness of monkeys and pigs." (Ref: Kanz-ul A'mal).

Nothing can be more damaging for the image of the Ulama than this sort of harsh and humiliating reproach recorded in Hadith in more than one narration.

In addition to the above narrations from Sahih Hadith severely condemning the Ulama (Madrasah-educated men), the Religious Leaders of old and the enlightened Intellectuals of modern Age are unanimous in their opinion that matters of Legal Reforms can not be left to the Madrasah-educated Ulama for consideration and disposal. The degree-holders of Madrasah system of education, having no Scientific background and no knowledge of current affairs are not adequately qualified for examining legal propositions suited to modern times, which may not be in tune with those considered appropriate for olden times. Therefore, the operation of Ijtihad can not be left to the Judgment of this class of Ulama.

Final Consideration:

The particulars of the views of different classes of Thinkers in the matter of qualification of persons deemed fit to operate the principle of Ijtihad have been examined elaborately above. The results may be summarised below:

(i) The orthodox standard of high education only in Islamic religious disciplines is not acceptable, because the standard does not satisfy the Qur'anic yard-stick of men of wisdom and understanding as discussed above.

(ii) The standard suggested by the Progressive Muslims is fairly close to the Qur'anic standard, and may be accepted as the second best, coming below the Quranic standard.

(iii) The Qur'anic standard of men who combine proficiency in Science and modern education with sincere adherence to the Faith and Practice of Islam, is evidently the best of the three standards under consideration.

To mention a specific example, a person of the type of Maulana Dr. Abdul Majid Daryabadi (1892-1977), who acquired equal competence in modern education and in Islamic Religious learning, is ideally suited for functioning as a Mujtahid. Other persons who qualify for operation of ijtihad may be those Degree-holders from Institutions such as Nadwatul-Ulama of Lucknow and the Faculty of Islamic Studies, Muslim University, Aligarh, provided the particular Scholar is noted for his personal character of honesty and integrity, and has acquired extensive awareness of World trends by systematic studies. Outside these academic circles, men of high secular education or profession who are known for sound knowledge and regular practive of Islamic discipline, combined with a character or honesty and integrity, are equally suitable for discharging the role of an Ijtihad Scholar in modern times.

The Ulama in general, though intelligent, highly educated in Religious lore and capable of social and even political leadership, are not educated in modernity, and fail to give a lead to the Community in the difficult task of confrontation with modernity, which has become unavoidable in the present-day World. Therefor, the Scholars, whose academic attainments are limited only to Medieval type of Education howsoever high, are considered unfit to practice Ijtihad in the present times of Scientific temper.

Qualification not to be Relaxed:

It must be noted that the enthusiam for ending the stagnation in Islamic Law System should not go to the extent of allowing Ijtihad to be performed by immature or under-qualified persons, or by persons, likely to be guided by whims and prejudice. Liberalisation has a tendency to act as an agent of disintegration. Ultra-zealous reformers may over-step the legitmate limits of legal authority in the absence of a judicious check on their excessive fervour. Departure from the principles under which Ijtihad is permissible, or lowering of qualifications from the level as rationalised and indicated above, will have harmful effect on the morale of Islamic Law, and may perhaps be sinful in the eyes of God.

The apprehension, however, is not that too often an over-zealous or under-qualified person will come forward to operate Ijtihad, but that persons satisfying the necessary requisite qualification may generally feel shy to undertake the responsibility. This may be due to shirking a valid responsibility, or to suffering from an inferiority complex or defeatist mentality. The attitude is not commendable and must be overcome, as the Community needs the sacrifice or service of good men to work and remove the stigma of the Community's utter backwardness in the context of rapid advancement by other World Communities.

Reference

R-1 : *Fundamentals of Ijtihad* by Maulana Taqi Amini, Idarah-e Adabiyat-e Dilli, Delhi-6, p.3.

R-2 : *The Religion of Islam* by Maulana Muhammad Ali, S. Chand & Co., New Delhi-55, p.115

R-3 : *Ijma and the Gate of Ijtihad* by Kemal A. Faruki, Gateway Publications, Karachi, 1954, p.8.

R-4 : *Saviours of Islamic Spirit, Vol.III* by Maulana Abul Hasan Ali Nadwi, Academy of Islamic Research and Publications, Lucknow-7, 1983, p.69.

R-5 : *Ulama* by Al-Haj Moinuddin Ahmed, Kitab Bhavan, New Delhi-2, 1990, p.78.

R-6 : *Saviours of Islamic Spirit, Vol.I* by Maulana Abul Hasan Ali Nadwi (Vide R-4), p.131.

R-7 : Ibid p.131.

R-8 : *Tazkirah* by Maulana Abul Kalam Azad, edited by Malik Ram, Sahitya Academy, 1968, pp.78, 79, 104.

R-9 : *Islam and the World* by Maulana Abul Hasan Ali Nadwi, Lucknow, 1973, p.108.

R-10 : Preface to R-1 above.

R-11 : *Muslim Personal Law* by Dr. Tahir Mahmood, All India Reporter, Ltd., Nagpur, 12, 1983, pp. 145-46.

R-12 : *Mishkat-ul Masabih, trans.* by Adbul Hamid Siddiqui, Kitab Bhavan, New Delhi-2, Vol.I, p. 154.

Section X

METHOD OF OPERATION

Old and New Mind:

Passing through Revolutions time and again, the modern World has finally emerged with new issues unthinkable a thousand years ago, needing solution to problems which the old mind shirks or is unable to tackle. Persons equipped with Medieval type of education develop an attitude which is subservient to antiquated norms relevant to that Age. They have not benefited themselves by possessing a free mind and widened outlook, which are the gifts of modern Scientific education. A mind which is accustomed to the knowledge of Caravans moving at 8 miles per hour or horse-drawn carts at 20 miles per hour, is not open to imagine or believe that light can travel 1,86,000 miles per second, or that man can ever land on the Moon.

Such is the gap between the two minds of that Age and this Age. The products of old School of Thought earn the credit of memorising the whole elaborate Text of the Holy Qur'an, or of reciting the same umpteen times in their lives, and yet they are not aware of its true spirit and teachings, and do not know that the Qur'an emphasises the study of Science three times more than the number of its exhortations for performance of prayers.

Men equipped with the mind, education and outlook of an Age long gone by, can not obviously steer the helm of affairs of the present Age. Muslims must now open their eyes to reality and not flatter themselves with a false sense of reverence for all olden things without discrimination. All that glitter may not be gold, and therefore the Holy Qur'an inspiringly says, *"So learn a lesson, O ye who have eyes!"* (59:2)

Beginning and Closure of Ijtihad:

The qualification for operation of Ijtihad which was in vogue during the earliest period, was the one which was set in motion by the holy Prophet himself. It was a simple and sensible proposition then, graphically illustrated by Hadith relating to the briefing of Hazrat Mu'az by the holy Prophet on the eve of his appointment as the Governor of Yemen. Approved by the Prophet, the matter was left to the wisdom of Hazrat Mu'az who outlined three steps for solution of all problems to be faced in the new Country of Yemen, just then added to the growing territory of Islam. According to him, the solution lay in considering the following aspects:

(i) Does the problem find a solution in the Injunctions of the Qur'an? If so, adopt it.

(ii) If not, look into Hadith to evolve a solution. If available, adopt it.

(iii) Failing to identify the problem with the directions in the Qur'an or Hadith, decide the matter according to own Judgment.

This is Ijtihad, fully legal and authoritative, according to the principle laid down by the Prophet. During the Prophet's life-time and thereafter, the Companions carried on the work accordingly. The four eminent Khulafa also took resort to Ijtihad whenever needed, in its simple and unostentatious form. There was no deviation or controversy.

If that was so fourteen hundred years back, who are the persons to be considered competent today to discharge the function of Ijtihad? For nearly three hundred years after the good old days of the holy Prophet, the Scholars qualified according to the Orthodox Standard were engaged in performing the task. Thereafter, the process was brought to an end in the Sunni World, while all the other sects of the Muslim community carried on the function for all time without any wrangling or controversy. The questions now arise:

(i) Could the process initiated by the holy Prophet himself be validly terminated by a group of non-Prophets? Section VII has examined the matter and concluded that the closure was neither valid nor wise.

(ii) If the process must be kept open, who are the persons considered competent in today's World to keep it running? Section IX has elaborately discussed and concluded that, not the men bearing qualification according to the Orthodox Standard, but the men declared wise and thoughtful by the Holy Qur'an should play the role.

(iii) What should be the mode of operation of the Ijtihad Legist of the 20th/21st Century?

Before attempting to answer the last item, a further glance at Questionnaire (ii) seems justified because the Orthodox qualification is quite respectable and high in a particular sense, and before dismissing it outright, it is worth looking into the *raison d'etre* of its unsuitability more searchingly.

Orthodox Standard no longer Relevant:

With the expansion of Islamic Empire, Countries having distinctive culture, administrative set-up, conflicting customs and practice, varying social conditions and life-patterns, raised new problems which required solutions to be dispensed with according to standardised Islamic principles. The Law-makers met the challenge by devising new approaches and novel methods of interpretation in order to formulate Rules appropriate to each new case.

After the Era of the first generation of Muslims, there were Scholars in large number participating in the process of Ijtihad and applying their mind to its operational principles. They elaborated and framed Rules relating to methods of elucidation, classification, inferences and deductions from foundational tenets of Islam. Generation after generation of Scholars kept themselves engaged in interpretation of Islamic legal provisions, gradually evolving new branches and sub-branches of the principles, and introducing new steps and formulae to arrive at operative orders.

The subsequent generation of Scholars claimed deeper insight and wider expertise in dealing with finer points and greater complexities of problems. The operational rules were then diversified and their application was made stiff and rigid. These rules were split up into sub-rules according to textual phraseology or connotation of terminology. In some cases, the substance of the proposition was distinguished as positive or negative in nature, upon which rested the classification of the proposition. Provision was also made for co-ordination of differences of opinion by different Scholars. Obviously, there was an element of ambition on the part of individual Scholars to gain reputation by propounding new approaches not thought of by others.

In this long process, a system of division of sentences, phrases and words as well as a chain of fresh terminologies were adopted. Sentences were divided into 4 classes, *Zahir, Nas, Mufassar, Muhkam,* and hidden notions into 4 classes, *Khafi, Mushkil, Mujmal, Mutashabih* while words were divided into 4 classes, *Haqiqah, Majaz, Sarih, Kinayah* and deductions or arguments were divided into 4 classes, *Ibarah, Isharah, Dalalah and Iqtiza.* There were many other terminologies, such as *Mafhum-e Muafiq, Mafhum-e Mukhalif, Mukhassas-e Am, Mukhassas-e Haisiyat* and scores of such other terse and abstruse deluge of technical terms.

As a sequel to the growing complexities and intricacies in the Theory and application of Ijtihad, the qualification of persons entitled to operate Ijtihad was raised to the maximum limit. It was held that such a person must be one of the top-most Scholars of the Age, a Philosopher, a Doctor of law possessing perfect perception and professional expertise. The practical effect of raising qualification so high was that no body with such a qualification was likely to be available, and so the process was doomed to come to an automatic halt.

A major stumbling block was then encountered when the Scholars of different Sectarian Schools namely, Hanafi, Maliki, Shafe'i, and Hanbali persisted in each one claiming his own decision to be correct even if it did not tally with others. The differences led to enunciation of conflicting rulings. By way of illustration, one case is mentioned below:

The Hanafi principle is not to eat meat of an animal slaughtered without reciting the name of God. But according to Shafe'i Hadith, such meat can be eaten. Once Hazrat Ayesha sought clarification from the Prophet in this matter and said, "People bring meat and we do not know whether they had recited the name of Allah. Can we eat it? The Prophet replied, *"Eat after reciting the name of Allah"*. (R-1).

Objects of Review:

The purpose of reviewing the situation in such elaborate details is to show how a simple legal provision initiated by the holy Prophet was twisted by later Scholars into a hundred complexities, all of which were not necessary, but were incorporated by ambitious Scholars anxious to earn a name. There is too much of pedantry, unnecessary show of learning and stiffness in prescribing norms, which made the whole process unworkable. In this connection, Shah Waliullah writes disapprovingly in his book *'Izalah'*, "People who were dispersed in different territories (after conquest by Ottoman Turks), took with them whatever they knew from their Juristic schools, and made it the basis of their Faith. What was before a deduced Code of life, now came to be regarded as a rigid creed and dogma. All their intellectual efforts were now concentrated on making deductions from deductions, and piling up details upon details." (R-2).

The consideration of above particulars may be held to be enough to arrive at Findings given below:

FINDING-A

Ijtihad was a simple and practical concept in the Prophet's time. The Scholars of Medieval Age changed it into a complicated and intricate legal axiom, defined by abstruse and pedantic expressions to indicate its scope and performance. By the 4th Century Hijri, the Law of Ijtihad suffered too much from hair-splitting, and was so tangled in a mess of Juristic formalities, and the qualification of the Ijtiahd Legist was raised so high that no honest Scholar ventured to undertake the performance. Ultimately some hardliners among Sunni Scholars closed the Gate of Ijtihad for all time to come, while the Scholars of other Islamic Sects did not agree. Voice of Protest began to be raised during all these Centuries against the Closure, but as the qualification of the Ijtihad Legist had not been rationalised and the old Orthodox Standard not formally declared unsuitable for the present Scientific Age, the stalemate continues. Whether the Orthodox Standard is appropriate in the modern Age, has been elaborately examined in the earlier Review, which finds it out-moded, time-worn and obsolete. This old-time system requires to be reconsidered, revised and replaced by a more sensible set of qualification.

FINDING-B

On the result of elaborate Review in Section IX, the selection of persons considered competent to exercise Ijtihad in modern times was finally confined to persons commended by the Holy Qur'an as *Ulu'l-amr* (men in authority), or *Ulu'l-albab* (men of Wisdom). Such persons are those that have acquired balanced proficiency in religious performance and Secular competence, with reputation for honesty and integrity. The Ijtihad Legist should be one such person.

Mode of Operation:

It is necessary to lay down the mode of operation of the Ijtihad Legist. The theme of the present publication relates mainly to creation of awareness about the urgency of opening the Gate of Ijtiahd. As such, the aspect of operational principles of the doctrine is strictly not within the scope of the present review. However, some brief and broad outlines are indicated below as the minimum working knowledge to enable the Ijtihad Legist to go ahead.

(i) Knowledge of Qur'an - The Ijtihad Legist should possess working knowledge of the fundamental legal sources of Islamic Law. As is well known, the Holy Qur'an is the first source of Islamic Law. The Legist is required to get acquainted with only some relevant Ayats, and not the whole of the Text of the Qur'an. There are altogether 6,360 Verses in the Book, out of which only about 250 Verses relate to matters of Law. In addition, there are about 200 other Verses which contain incidental light reference to legal notions. It may not be a difficult task to study these limited number of Verses and learn about their implications. Some books in Urdu and English are available which may facilitate study of Qur'anic Laws and Islamic Jurisprudence. At the end of this publication, a list of "Books for Further Study" may be seen for reference.

(ii) Knowledge of other sources - next to the Qur'an, the other sources of Islamic Laws are Hadith, Ijma and Qiyas. There are publications in Urdu and English on Hadith literature. There are also useful books on Fiqh (Islamic Jurisprudence). It is necessary to grasp the essence of these sources of Law.

'Hedaya' and *Fatawa Alamgiri'* which are available in Arabic, Urdu, and English are standard books on Fiqh for Hanafi Muslims. They are helpful for understanding the legal aspects of the Qur'an and Sunnah. Moreover, the compilation *'Shami'* of Damascus in the 18th Century, is also authoritative, and in some cases, it had changed the rulings of *Fatawa Alamiri.*

(iii) Knowledge of Terminologies - It is also necessary for the Legist to understand and work out the 3-tier legal structure mentioned below:

'Usul' (root)- This is the fundamental legal provision;

'Furu' (Branch) - signifies applied law;
'Fatwa' (Verdict) - Expression of final opinion in specific cases.

Practical Working:

The Ijtihad Legist has to undertake two types of Law-making work, namely, interpretation of old Rulings and formulation of new rulings on fresh problems.

Old Rulings:

Rulings which are already in existence but appear to have become unsuited to the spirit of present time, require consideration with utmost respect for the old notion which has served the Community for Centuries in the past, but seems to have lost apparent relevance today. It is necessary to pay attention to the necessity of its adoption to new circumstances. The following guidelines of operation should prove helpful:

(i) The problem under consideration may be solved in most cases through sensible interpretation of some key words contained in the old rulings. As a result, the old rulings will continue to stand intact without any change in their form of expression, while they would be rendered compatible with modern conditions on the basis of only intelligent interpretation.

(ii) Arabic vocabulary is highly elastic and meaningful. The literal structure of *'Usul'* forming essence of the Law is often capable of yielding the desired connotation through apt lexical exercise. No change in the literal form of the Law may be necessary.

(iii) The Qur'an is not averse to change when considered necessary according to the spirit of Verse 13: 11. If adaptation to modern conditions is necessary without offending the provisions of the Qur'an and Hadith, the ruling may be subjected to necessary change in literal structure.

(iv) If the entire structure of Ruling requires replacement by a new set of expression, this may be carefully done only when there is no clear Injunction in the Scriptures on the subject, and when there is no corresponding Ijma of early generation of Muslims to cover the problem.

(v) An old ruling may be altered or cancelled when the 'illa' or reason deduced from Shariah no longer exists or has changed.

New Rulings:

The Ijtihad Legist may formulate new rulings on contemporary problems on which there is complete silence in the Qur'an and Sunnah, or in any reliable Ijma. Thorough care must be taken to ensure that the language and import of the new ruling are not repugnant to any of the provisions of the sacred Scriptures.

Maulana Muhammad Ali says, "The sphere of Ijtihad is a very wide one, since it seeks to fulfil all the requirements of the Muslim Community, which are not met with expressly in the Holy Qur'an and Hadith." (R-3). Such requirements may therefore be met by the process of Ijtihad exercised judiciously. The intention in formulating new rulings should be only for the benefit of the Muslim Community, and not for the advantage of any group or individual. It is the personal responsibility of the Ijtihad Legist to ensure this condition.

Authority and Privileges of Ijtihad Legist:

The Ijtihad Legist must know that he has considerable

authority in his own field. He has got the powers to disregard, revoke or replace the legal decisions contained in the Standard Works of Fiqh under certain circumstances. Rulings which are not based on clear Injunctions of the Qur'an and Hadith, and also Ijmas which have not been concluded on the basis of the Qur'an and Hadith, may be cancelled or changed by the present day Ijtihad Legist. Moreover, a change in *'illa'* is a ground for alteration or cancellation of the old ruling. (R-4).

As regards the privileges of Ijtihad Legist, he may have a measure of satisfaction if he sincerely and diligently performs the task because of the element of benignity inherent in the system of Islamic Law. There are three favourable considerations:

(a) *Sahih Bokhari* lays down *(Vol.II, Kitab-ul Itisam)* that there is twice the reward if Ijtihad is performed correctly, and only one reward even if the work is done incorrectly but sincerely.

(b) If the decision of the Ijtihad Legist becomes different from that of another Scholar, both the viewpoints are upheld under the principle of *'Ikhtilaf'* if there is proof of sincerity behind the effort.

(c) In case the Ijtihad Legist arrives at a wrong decision after hard and intelligent efforts, no discredit is implicated to him.

In conclusion, the Ijtihad Legist has the authority to keep the Islamic Laws fresh from time to time by exercise of the function of Ijtihad, subject to the condition that the principles laid down in the Qur'an and Hadith are not contravened in any manner. He enjoys the honour and respect arising from the privileges accorded to him by provisions of Hadith, as also from his personal virtues of learning and character.

Reference

R-1 : *Bukhari, Muslim,* Chapter on *Assaidwazahaaih;* also *Fundamentals of Ijtihad* by M. Taqi Amini, Idarah-e Adabiyat-e Delli, Delhi, 1986, p.68.

R-2 : *A Short History of the Revivalist Movement in Islam* by Maulana Abul A'la Maududi, Markazi Maktaba Islami, Delhi-6, 1973, p.75.

R-3 : *The Religion of Islam,* by Maulana Muhammad Ali, S. Chand & Co., New Delhi-55, p.103.

R-4 : *Ijma and the Gate of Ijtihad* by Kemal A. Faruki, Gateway Publications, Karachi, 1954, p.8.

Section XI

CONCLUDING OBSERVATIONS

Islam and Science:

The Qur'an's interest in Science is well-known. The Holy Book makes it obligatory for men to study and wonder at the Divine Scheme of Creation of all that exists from the Heavens down to the core of the Earth. *Surah Luqman* presents a consistent logic, inducing men to ponder and reflect over the natural phenomena and mysteries of God's wonderful creations. It commends men to do so in order to enable them to comprehend the Majesty and Sublimity of Divine attributes of God and His infinite Powers of creativity. Science and Religion have no conflict in Islam. Both are *ipso facto* two different ways of comprehension of one common motif - the Reality inherent in Divinity.

The Qur'an rightly emphasises performance of righteous deeds together with remembrance of God. But it is remarkable that the Qur'an's insistence on acquisition of Scientific competence is more pronounced and more frequent than its exhortations for religious performance. The total number of Verses in the Qur'an is 6,247 and if the 113 Nos. of Bismillah Verses with which Surahs open, are included, the number rises to 6,360. Out of this number, only 200 Verses ordain observance of religious performance and 250 Verses relate to Islamic laws, while as many as 750 Verses emphasise the study and culture of Scientific Knowledge relating to Secular Science. Dr. Muhammad Aijazul Khatib of Damuscus University says,

"In contrast to 250 Verses which are legislative, some 750 Verses of the Holy Qur'an, almost one-eighth of it, exhort Believers to study Nature; to reflect, to make the best use of Reason and to make the Scientific enterprise an integral part of the Community's life". (R-1). This learned Professor, like a multitude of other modern intellectuals, strongly urges Muslims to take to the study of Science and Technology in all earnestness.

Consistent with the Holy Qur'an's explicit exhortations for study of Science, there are oft-repeated counsels of Wisdom emphasised by the holy Prophet regarding the peremtoriness in acquiring Scientific Knowledge. A few important sayings of the Prophet may be seen in Appendix-A.

Despite the clamour for more and more of Western Science and Technology to be infused into the blood and veins of Muslims all over the World, there is a growing awareness among the thinking section that if Islam has to play a sensible and leading role over the latest World trends, keeping its individuality intact, the position has to be considered judiciously and a correct line of behaviour has to be evolved to delineate a new course that may achieve the double object of wiping out the stagnation of Muslim mind on the one hand, and avoid the impasse and dilemma which the Western Civilization has come to face embarrassingly today, on the other hand.

The Western mind is dominated today by Science in its raw and rigorous form, utterly devoid of moral values. Imitation of such an unrighteous Science-ridden character, unless adequately refined by application of Qur'anic Wisdom may lead the groping Muslims to an unenviable blind alley. In order to get the maximum benefit from the achievements of modern Science combined with the heritage of Islamic culture, a suitable appliance is necessary with a view to blend the two into one rational norm capable of satisfying the requirements of the present times. Ijtihad is that appropriate appliance, which duly revived and re-applied to the problems of the Islamic Society and Polity, will achieve the ideal blending of the gifts of modern Science and the Wisdom of the Holy Qur'an.

God's Changing Universe:

God's Universe is dynamic. It is always moving, growing and changing. It is vast, so vast that the light of some stars travelling at a speed of 1,86,000 miles per second has not reached the Earth yet during millions of years of its existence. The Universe, and all its phenomena are changing. The Space, the Time, the Matter and all objects of Divine creation are changing. The Book of God, the Law of God, the Commandments of God and everything created by God are changing. Man is changing. The Human Society is changing. The Laws and rules governing the Human Society are changing. Only God and nothing else remains unchanged. God is One Who is immutable. All the rest are mutable or changeful, including the religious laws ordained by God - the Shariah, the Ijma as well as Ijtihad. If Ijtihad has been closed, rightly or wrongly, the decision of closure may also change if there are sensible grounds to do so.

Ijtihad a Benign Godsend:

In this changeful World, some sort of provision was necessary to hold man steady in fulfillment of life's purpose while inspiring him to keep pace with the flight of time. That precious provision was wisely designed by the holy Prophet in the form of Ijtihad, which was evolved within the frame-work of Islamic Law.

During the early Centuries of the Hijri Calendar, the Prophet, the great Imams and numerous learned religious leaders frequently took resort to the process of Ijtihad, thereby judiciously providing missing links in the body of Islamic Laws. The varying needs of succeeding generations, the multitude of requirements of different Countries and the conflicting heritage of many races merging into the streams of Islamic Brotherhood, could be met harmoniously and continuously by the elastic provision of Ijtihad. Ijtihad thus served as a great blessing for the growth and integration of the World Muslim Society.

Ijtihad Era - the Golden Age of Islam:

All great Nations of the World had a span of their golden Age at some time or other. The Egyptians had their Age of Pyramids, the Greeks had their Periclean Era and the Romans had their Augustan Period. Similarly, the Islamic World had its epoch of Glory. The duration of the first three Centuries of Islamic History, corresponding to what may be termed as the *'Ijtihad Era'*, is hailed as the Golden Age of Islamic Culture and Civilization. During the Umayyad Caliphate (661-750 AD), the Muslims began to leap into the future greatness of the Islamic Commonwealth. Thereafter, during the Abbaside Regime (750-1258 AD), the Muslims established themselves as the custodian and patron of Knowledge and Learning of the World. Every part of the Globe was intensively searched and exploited by them for retrieval of the hoarded treasure of ancient wisdom and genius. The gains were brought to a resplendent World Centre at Baghdad, and then utilised in building Universities and International Libraries, free to every seeker of Knowledge and learning. In these Centres of Intellectual pursuit, great Philosophers, Scientists and Pioneers such as Galen, Dioscorides, Aristotle, Plato, Euclid, Ptolemy and other Classical Scholars were studied side by side with the Qur'an.

As a result of the initiative and dash in the field of intellectual creativity, the Muslims distinguished themselves as Leaders of the Political World, Teachers of spiritual regeneration, Harbingers of Scientific advancement and Torch-bearers of Civilization. This was a brilliant epoch when new avenues of Knowledge in Literature, Philosophy, Science and Arts were opened by renowned master-minds born in the Commonwealth of Islam. The period saw the birth of eminent Chemists, Algebraists, Physicians, Clinicians, Mathematicians, Physicists, Chronologists, Astronomers, Historians and Geographers among different Muslim Nations.

Of the several factors responsible for the series of momentous intellectual and cultural contributions to World Civilization by the talent and vigour of Muslim mind, the most notable element was the provision of Ijtihad, so wisely formulated and implemented by the holy Prophet. It worked as the fountain-head of expediency and a masterpiece of ingenuity, necessary for mankind to find ways and means at every turn and pass, which Islam had to encounter.

Rise of Western Nations:

With all the grand History behind the Muslims, they started sliding down the ladder of affluence and prosperity from the 13th Century A.D. The newly emerging Renaissance Movement of Western Europe generated a series of material and intellectual incentives, specially in the fields of Science and Technology, and made European Countries independent of Islamic influence which had dominated the civilized World for most part of the Medieval Age.

Events of paramount importance began to stir man's

imagination. Countless Scientists, Discoverers and Inventors worked hard to create a new World in place of the old. Colossal Scientific advancements and daring adventures brought about a new phase of Civilization. Explorers like Columbus and Vasco da Gama transformed the vast Ocean from a dreadful, forbidden expanse into a profitable commercial highway. The tribe of Scientists like Copernicus, Galileo, Newton and Faraday unfolded the secrets of Nature and harnessed them to man's growing needs. Geniuses like Volta and Galvani in Physics, Priestley, Davy and La Voisier in Chemistry, and Linne and Wolff in Biology enriched their respective Sciences and gave rise to new theories about the Universe and man. The result of researches by Quisney, Adam Smith and Malthus added new dimensions to the Science of Economics. The birth of Rousseau, Voltaire, Montesquieu, Darwin, Goethe and a legion of other eminent men had far-reaching effects on Literature, Religion, Philosophy, Politics and other Social Sciences. The space adventures of Armstrong broke the myth of the Moon, which had been venerated as a symbol of Beauty and Elegance. Space was annihilated by Speed. Remote transmission and control of Sound and Vision became instantaneous. Unexpected disasters were prevented by Electronic warning systems. And many more such grand events came in crowded succession to change the face of the Globe.

The Western Intellectuals fearlessly criticised and assailed the thoughts and conventions of the Classical World, and laid the foundation of a new World of perception an imagination. The World began to change at a breath-taking pace. The destiny of the World was thus cast in the West. The World leadership was taken over by the Western Nations.

In this process, the Muslims lost contact with the

rapidly developing West, and got no share in the vast treasure of Scientific Knowledge and Technical skill that the West evolved during the course of Centuries after the Renaissance. The Western nations gained supremacy because they adopted the principles of acting on Reason, welcoming newness and looking forward, while the Muslims continued to remain stagnant because they became prone to prefer dogma to Reason, to detest newness and to look to bygone days.

Decline of Muslims in all Spheres:

Today, the Muslim Society has reduced itself to a state of debasement and backwardness in the context of swift progress and advancement in the contemporary scene. A curtain of poverty and ignorance has descended on the face of the Community, segregating it in all walks of life from the advanced Nations of the World. The Muslim Society is now known for its inner strife, division, self-contradiction, as well as for its wars between Muslims and Muslims, its threat to World Peace, its excessive wealth somewhere and excessive poverty else where. On Political front the Muslims are divided, in economic field they are under-developed, and in Religio-cultural sphere, illiteracy, ignorance and lack of earnestness have driven them into a blind alley. Steeped in superstition, mentally imprisoned by dogmas, governed in daily life by customs and usages prescribed over a thousand years back, the Muslim is considered to be the *'Sickman'* of the World today.

The on-rushing advent of the 21st Century is rife with new attitudes. Whether it is the field of Education, Economic pursuit, Political activities, Social relations, Industrial enterprise or even Religious practice, new ways of thinking have lent their indelible colour. Diversification of Knowledge on Secular, Scientific and technical disciplines has induced fresh frame of mind and promoted fresh urge for novelties, enabling the present generation to play a more constructive role in the march of Mankind to unlimited progress.

At this critical juncture, the Muslims have coiled themselves inside narrow parochial shells. They refuse to open their eyes and look forward to the irresistible forces of the coming times. They are content to look backwards to the old-time affairs of past Centuries, as if it were possible to draw inspiration therefrom for all the new varieties of performance in the 20th and 21st Centuries. Their habit of looking backward for everything in life has decimated their capacity to look forward even in matters of benefit available under the new dispensation. Their mind has suffered from mental degeneration followed by intellectual sterility, giving way to obscurantism inherent in the Doctrine of Taqlid.

The deplorable state of Muslim mind and attitude may primarily be the result of influence of the antiquated and inappropriate type of education imparted by Madrasahs. Such a system of out-moded education prevails not only in Indian Madrasahs, but also in the Madrasahs of many Countries predominantly populated by Muslims. An author of international repute, V.S. Naipaul of West Indies, who has been recently knighted by the British Government and is now being considered for a Nobel Prize in Literature, visited a number of Muslim Countries, Iran, Pakistan, Malaysia and Indonesia, and took stock of local conditions including the system of Education given in Islamic Madrasahs. He has recorded his impression of the effect of such education in his book 'Among the Believers' in his characteristic witty and terse style, *"The poor teaching the poor to be poor"* (R-2).

With such ill-conceived education which neither contributes to intellectual development nor adds to economic potentiality of Muslim boys and girls receiving education in "Islamic" Madrasahs, it is futile to expect vigour of mind and strength of character necessary to face the new challenges of the present and coming times.

The incomprehension by Muslim mind about the threat from new forces and the consequent failure in acquiring adaptability to new conditions, may result in the collapse of their Community's total image. They may then be ignominiously left behind other World Communities to lead an unenviable life and no more to be counted as equals to respectable Citizens of the World.

FACTORS LEADING TO DECLINE

(A)-Closing the Gate of Ijtihad:

Subsequent to the brilliant epoch of the four great Imams, no Ulama of outstanding talent were born in the Community. The standard of law-making declined as the later Ulama got involved in mutual discrimination and rivalry. Sectarianism gradually crept into their head and heart. Feelings of frustration arose as no body hoped for recognition of their withering talent. At this stage, an Ijma-e Ummat was supposed to have been convened about the 4th Century Hijri, terminating the process of Ijtihad in the Sunni Sect. No fresh thinking was allowed thereafter.

The closure of Ijtihad alone, however, was not responsible for the all-round deterioration in the Muslim Society. There were a number of other inherent causes leading to the decline in moral and material spheres. The period of Islamic History subsequent to the invasion of the Mongols resulting in the downfall of the Abbasides, and even a little earlier than that, was a period of intense Political intrigues. There was lack of seriousness of purpose in individual life, made worse by sectarian and religious in-fighting. In this great confusion, some distinct trends found suitable climate to flourish, as mentioned below:

(B)-Influence of Taqlid:

The winding up of the process of Ijtihad acted as a stimulus to the Doctrine of Taqlid. People could look back to precedents, but could not advocate any new type of thinking or introduce any innovation. This temperament amounted to thoughtless veneration for old order of things. It killed incentive for intellectualism necessary for acquisition of modern Scientific Knowledge which is essential for progress and development of mankind. The Doctrine of Taqlid tabooed all progressive ideas. Scientific education was discouraged or considered not necessary in the interest of conservation of true Islamic Culture and Tradition.

(C)-Growth of Sufism:

The Philosophy of Sufism began to be eulogised, preached and practised extensively about this time. It induced a spirit of looking beyond the earthly life, and of discouragement of Worldly responsibilities. The best brains within the Community were increasingly inducted into this philosophical pursuit, making room for men of lesser talent and ability to run the Administration and other worldly affairs. The result was an inevitable decline in all spheres of Worldly activities.

(D)-Awakening of other Communities:

The vacuum created by the Muslims withdrawing from the fields of Command and Action, induced other world Communities to step in. These Communities had just emerged from the Dark Age as a result of Muslims disseminating learning and enlightenment all over the known World of that Age. They acquired the knowledge and proficiency necessary for taking over the World of Culture and Civilization that the Muslims had built, and then marched ahead in successive strides, till the Western Nations came to rule over all other Nations of the World, including the Muslim Nations themselves.

The decline of Muslims in all fields of activity from the 13th Century A.D. forms a sad Chapter of Islamic History. Although there were occasional flashes of revival thereafter, as evident from the great Empire-building by Iranian Safvis, Indian Moghuls and Osmani Turks, the process of persistent decline was so deeply ingrained in Muslim blood and veins that the Community as a whole was destined to descend to the lower rungs of the international ladder of the 20th Century.

It will appear that a number of factors as mentioned above was responsible for this tragedy, the chief among which was the closure of the Gate of Ijtihad. This unwise decision led to the serious consequences of denial of individual rights of Muslims to exercise their own Judgment and to place reliance on Reason. The ban on Ijtihad also induced Muslims to look backward to the 7th Century for deriving guidance for action in the 20th Century and ever thereafter, rather than to look forward to the 21st Century and to seek inspiration from the expanding horizon of Scientific Knowledge and generous Learning. The habit of looking back as a matter of principle led to the tendency of vain glory over past greatness instead of serious efforts to enrich the past heritage and to harness it in meeting the new challenges to attain future greatness. This pernicious habit has been at the root of continuing torpor and stagnation of the Muslim Community.

The Decree of closure, a Hoax:

Dr. Iqbal, with all his earnestness in the process of

reconstructing Islamic Ideals, discovered that "the closing of the Gate of Ijtihad is a pure fiction". (R-3). The study made in the present publication has concluded that the closure of Ijtihad was the irresponsible work of a band of frustrated Ulama of no good talent, belonging to the 4th Century Hijri or thereafter, when the visible signs of all-round decadence had begun to demoralise the character and disposition of the Ummah. In fact, the closure of Ijtihad was a hoax played with ulterior motives, and has no scriptural validity. It is deplorable that this unholy game was not discovered earlier, and if discovered by some, was not pressed to the point of being declared null and void. In the absence of any such firm action, the Decree of Closure persisted all these long Centuries, causing incalculable harm and killing the spirit of creativity and aspiration for advancement within the Muslim Community.

Now, however, since the mischief has been confirmed after a comprehensive study and investigation, and since hundreds of Intellectuals and Religious Leaders have been strongly advocating the opening of the Gate of Ijtihad, no time should be lost any longer in apprising all quarters that the Closure of Ijtihad is not valid, and is treated as null and void forthwith, and further that the operation of Ijtihad is open for exercise according to approved guidelines.

Ijtihad as the Saviour:

The task of retrieval of Muslims from the abysmal depths of backwardness in all spheres of life is riddled with dilemma. Far from trying to achieve progress and advancement now open for all sections of the people, the Muslims are not even willing to open their eyes to see if they are backward at all. They do not realise that their condition is unenviable, urgently needing a change for the better. Their Religious Leaders have not taught them the significance of the sacred Qur'anic Verse:

إِنَّ اللّٰهَ لَا يُغَيِّرُ مَا بِقَوْمٍ
حَتّٰى يُغَيِّرُوا مَا بِأَنْفُسِهِمْ

Meaning- *"Verily, Allah changeth not the condition of a people until they (first) change their conditions by themselves".*

-Holy Qur'an: *Surah Ar-Ra'd* 13:11-

Islam has the wisdom to anticipate that with the passage of time, the people will stand in need of a legal provision to enable them to keep their rules and laws uptodate, and to maintain freshness in outlook at all times. Ijtihad is that wise provision, which had stood the test of time during the early Centuries of Islamic Era. In the present Age, when the Muslim Community is afflicted with decline and retrogression for over a thousand years, Ijtihad is expected to serve as an effective weapon to cure the cancer of illiteracy, inaction, immobility and diffidence, which ail the Muslim Society all over the World.

Ijtihad was necessary even in the formative days of the Prophet, when man's World was small, social problems were few and the statecraft was simple. It should all the more be necessary now, when every aspect of life has become complex and problematic, and the Muslims feel confused, bewildered and frustrated. The lesson learnt from Islamic History points to the fact that Ijtihad had led to intellectual creativity so long it was kept in operation, and its closure has led to all round stagnation for the last several Centuries.

The benefits expected to accrue by adoption of the Doctrine of Ijtihad at the present unpredictable times are so vital and indispensable that if such a Doctrine had never existed in the past, it should now be urgently necessary to formulate and adopt it to serve as a panacea for the ailments of the present-day life of Muslims. Adoption of Ijtihad will save the coming generation of Muslims from developing a sense of contempt for their recent past and a feeling of despair for their remote future. Islam can then regain its former dynamic and creative character by liberating Muslims from the fetters of their own making.

Under the contemporary conditions, Ijtihad is imperative and calls for immediate action. Its Legist must be the right type of person available in the Society. The view that persons with the highest comprehensive Knowledge of Qur'an, Hadith and Islamic Jurisprudence only are entitled to operate Ijtihad, has already been exploded. There is no indication anywhere in the Qur'an or Hadith that a person who is noted for high proficiency only in the abstruse religious literature and rigid religious performance, but is not either honest or truthful, or is not well-versed in secular education and in present day affairs, should be the proper man to be consulted in times of war or peace. A person with one-sided qualification, leaning heavily on Theology and Jurisprudence and unfamiliar with the indispensable wealth of latest Knowledge of Science and human affairs, is not the right type of Ijtihad Legist now required.

The right type of Ijtihad Legist, as considered after elaborate examination of all aspects made earlier, is the person who is good in Knowledge and practice of Islamic Faith, proficient in secular education and current World trends, and is reputed for honesty and integrity of character. It may not be too difficult to locate such an eligible person in the contemporary Society.

Face the 21st Century Wisely:

As the 21st Century is rapidly approaching, there are unmistakable indications of profound changes increasingly coming to influence human affairs. The effect of unlimited Scientific advancement is bound to stir up man's imagination. Wisdom and sense of anticipation of the Western Nations have led them to adopt new life-styles by way of adaptability to changing conditions. But the Muslims, who have failed for long to keep pace with the progress of time, still remain unconcerned. They may enable themselves to rise and to live as honourable citizens of the World if only they adjust themselves to the changing tune of time. Such adjustments are possible by application of the principle of Ijtihad to the newly arising circumstances of life liable to be encountered in the immediate present and in the coming new Century.

There is therefore no issue before the Islamic World today more urgent than to get adjusted with the irresistible changes of the coming times, if further ignominy in the contemporary Society is to be avoided. Those who will not learn from hard experience of the past, and will not benefit by intelligent anticipation of the future, are doomed to face oblivion. Reliance on Reason and far-sightedness and keeping an open mind, helped by the process of Ijtihad to ensure freshness and compatibility with Islamic values at all times, will help the Muslims to rise to the desired level. If they do not acquire the necessary sense of discernment even at this late stage, they may have no choice but to eat the crumbs of bread left over the banquet tables of Western Nations.

Reference

R-1 : *The Review of Religions* for April, 1984 (European Edition), published by London Mosque, London, p.30.

R-2 : *Among The Believers* by V.S. Naipaul, Penguin Books, Great Britain, 1983, p.304.

R-3 : *The Reconstruction of Religious Thought in Islam* by Dr. Sir Muhammad Iqbal, Kitab Publishing House, Delhi-6, 1974, p.178.

APPENDIX-A

Sayings of the holy Prophet in exhortation of study of Science and acquisition of Knowledge.

(Ref: *The Spirit of Islam* by Syed Ameer Ali, Methuen & Co. London, 1965, page 362-63).

---

* One hour's meditation on the Work of the Creator is better than seventy years of prayer.

* To listen to the instructions of Science and Learning for one hour is more meritorious than attending the funerals of a thousand Martyrs, and more meritorius than standing up in prayer for a thousand nights.

* To listen to the words of the Learned, and to instil into the heart the lessons of Science, is better than religious exercises, better than emancipating a hundred slaves.

* Seek Knowledge even unto China.

* The ink of the Scholar is more holy than the blood of the Martyr.

* The Seeker of Knowledge will be greeted in Heaven with a welcome from the Angels.

* He who leaves his home in search of Knowledge, walks in the path of God.

* He who travels in search of Knowledge, to him God shows the way to Paradise.

To the Student who goes forth in quest of Knowledge, God will allot a high place in the Mansions of Bliss.

APPENDIX-B

Letter of Authority No. 385/Jeem dated 1-4-1411 Hijri, issued by Dar-ul Ifta of Dar-ul Uloom, Deoband (U.P.)

سوالات

(۱) اجتہاد کی بندش کا فیصلہ کس سال میں اور کس مقام میں ہوا ؟

(۲) علماء یا فقہاء جنھوں نے اجماعِ اُمت کی رہنمائی کی اور اجتہاد کی بندش جاری کی اُن بزرگوں کے اسمائے گرامی اور تعریف کیا ہیں ؟

۳۸۵
ج

جواب

علیکم السلام ورحمۃ اللہ وبرکاتہ

باسمہ سبحانہٗ

الجواب وباللہ التوفیق

سرخیل جماعت اہل حق حضرت مولانا شاہ ولی اللہ محدث دہلوی رحمۃ اللہ علیہ مقلدین وغیر مقلدین دونوں ہی کے بڑے اور دونوں ہی کے نزدیک معتمد و معتبر ہیں ۔

وہ اپنی معرکۃ الآرا کتاب الانصاف میں تحریر فرماتے ہیں:۔

فالمذهب للمجتهدين سرٌ الهمه الله تعالیٰ العلماء وجمعهم

عليه من حيث يشعرون اولا يشعرون۔

(الانصاف ص۶۲ مع ترجمہ)

ترجمہ:۔ حاصل یہ کہ مذہب مجتہدین کی پابندی ایک راز ہے جس کو اللہ تعالیٰ نے علماء کے دل میں ڈالا اور ان کو اس پر متفق کیا۔ خواہ وہ اس کو جانیں یا نہ جانیں۔

یعنی یہ اجماع عملی ہے۔ اجماع قولی نہیں ہے کہ آپ کے دونوں سوالوں میں سے کوئی سوال متوجہ ہو اور اجماع عملی بڑھا ہوا ہوتا ہے اجماع قولی سے، اس لئے کہ اجماع قولی کا مآل بھی وہی اتحاد فی العمل ہوتا ہے جو اجماع عملی پر ہے۔ نیز یہ اجماع عملی اللہ تبارک کے رازوں میں سے ایک راز ہے۔ امت کی حفاظت اور گمراہی سے بچانے کے لئے اللہ تعالیٰ نے دوسری صدی کے بعد علمائے حق کے قلب پر الہام فرمادیا اور سب علمائے حق اس اتحاد و اجماع پر متحد و مجتمع ہو گئے۔ اور امت محمدیہؐ کے اسی امن و حفاظت کے ماتحت تقلید شخصی بھی از خود وجود میں آگئی اور وہ بھی اسی الہام برحق کی جنس سے ہے۔ اس کو بھی حضرت شاہ صاحب نے اسی کتاب کے صفحہ۷ میں فرمایا ہے کہ جب ہندوستان میں علمائے احناف کے علاوہ مالکی، شافعی، حنبلی علماء موجود نہ ہوں تو یہاں کے لوگوں پر امام ابوحنیفہ کی تقلید واجب ہے۔

اور اس حقیقت کی جانب ارشادات رسول علیہ السلام میں بھی اشارات موجود ہیں۔ کما اشار الیہ هذا الحدیث ایضاً۔

عن ابی ہریرۃؓ قال قال رسول اللہ صلی اللہ علیہ وسلم یتعاقبون فیکم ملائکۃ باللیل وملائکۃ بالنہار (الی آخر الحدیث) (مشکوٰۃ شریف باب فضائل الصلوات وھکذا فی البخاری ومسلم)

حضرت شیخ عبدالحق محدث صاحبؒ ملائکہ کے اس آنے وجانے کی حکمت بتلاتے ہیں۔ بقولہ برائے ضبط احوال بندگان و دربرداشتن اعمال ایناں۔ وقال صاحب الفتح تحت ھذا الحدیث وفیہ الاخبار بما نحن فیہ من ضبط احوالنا الخ اور ہمارے احوال واعمال کے ضبط وانتظام کا اعلیٰ فرد دین حنیف کی حفاظت وانتظام کا ہمارے اندر پیدا ہوتا بھی ہے اور اسی کا الہام اللہ تعالیٰ اس اجماع عملی کے ذریعہ سے علمائے حق کے قلوب میں ڈالا اور چل پڑا۔

واللہ تعالیٰ اعلم

العبد نظام الدین غفرلہٗ

مفتی دارالعلوم دیوبند

۱؍۴؍سنہ ۱۴۱۱ھ

الجواب صحیح
حبیب الرحمٰن عفا اللہ عنہٗ

الجواب صحیح
کفیل الرحمٰن

BIBLIOGRAPHY

1. Books for further Study

Aksi Qur'an Majeed Mutarjam (Arabic-Urdu), Tr. and Comm. by Maulana Ashraf Ali Thanawi, Farid Book Depot, Delhi-6

Qur'anic Laws by Muhammad Valibhai Merchant, Kitab Bhavan, New Delhi.

Meanings of Sahih Bokhari (Arabic-English), Tr. into English by Dr. Muhammad Muhsin Khan, Kitab Bhavan, New Delhi.

The Hedaya, 2 Vols. Tr. by Charles Hamilton (T. Bensley, London), re-print at New Delhi.

Fatawa Alamgiri, 4 Vols. (Urdu), by Maulana Auzar Shah, Deoband, U.P.

Al-Hadis by Al-Haj Maulana Fazlul Karim, Book Agency, Baithak Khana Road, Calcutta.

Principles of Mahomedan Law by Sir D.F. Mulla, 18th Edition, N.M. Tripathi, Bombay

Mahomedan Law, 2 Vols. by Justice Syed Ameer Ali, Calcutta, 1929.

Muhammadan Jurisprudence by Sir Abdur Rahim, Madras, 1911.

Islamic Jurisprudence in the Modern World by A. A. Qadri, N. M. Tripathy, Bombay.

II. General Reference

Ahmed, Al-Haj Moinuddin,
ULAMA, (Kitab Bhavan, New Delhi, 1990).

Ali, Allama Abdullah Yusuf,
THE MEANING OF THE CLORIOUS QUR'AN, (Dar-al Kitab Al-Misri, Cairo, Lahore Edn. 1934).

Ali, Maulana Muhammad,
THE RELIGION OF ISLAM, (S. Chand & Co., New Delhi, 1981).

Ali, Syed Ameer,
A SHORT HISTORY OF THE SARACENS, (Kitab Bhavan, New Delhi, 1977).

Ali Syed Ameer,
THE SPIRIT OF ISLAM, (Methuen, London, 1965).

Amini, Maulana Taqi,
FUNDAMENTALS OF IJTIHAD, (Idarah-e Adabiyat-e Dilli, Delhi-6).

Arsh, Malsiani,
ABUL KALAM AZAD, (Publications Division, G/I, New Delhi).

Athar Hussain,
THE GLORIOUS CALIPHATE, (Academy of Islamic and Publications, Lucknow).

Atta, Dr. Mohyuddin,
ABU BAKR, (S. Chand & Co. Ram Nagar, New Delhi).

Azad, Maulana Abul Kalam,
THE TARJUMAN al-QUR'AN Vol. I. Tr. by Dr. Syed Abdul Latif, Asia Publishing House, Bombay.

Daryabadi, Maulana Dr. Abdul Majid,
TAFSIR-ul QUR'AN, 4 Vols., (Taj Publishers, Bombay, 1981).

Dilip Hiro,
ISLAMIC FUNDAMENTALISM, (Paladin, London).

Faruki, Kemal A.,
IJMA AND GATE OF IJTIHAD, (Gateway Publications, Karachi, 1954).

Fyzee, A. A. A.,
A MODERN APPROACH TO ISLAM, (Asia).

Gandhi, Raj Mohan,
EIGHT LIVES, (Roli Books International, 1986).

Ghazali, Imam,
IHYA ULOOM ID-DIN, Tr. by Maulana Fazlul Karim, (Kitab Bhavan, New Delhi, 1982).

Gibb, H. A. R.,
ISLAM, (Oxford University Press, London).

Guillaume, Alfred,
ISLAM, (Penguine, 1964).

Hanifi, M. Jamil,
ISLAM AND THE TRANSFORMATION OF CULTURE, (Asia Publishing House, Bombay, 1974).

Hasan, Dr. Ahmad,
THE DOCTRINE OF IJMA IN ISLAM, Islamic Research Institute, Islamabad, Pakistan, 1984

Haykal, Muhammad Husayn,
THE LIFE OF MUHAMMAD, (North American Trust Publications, Re-printed by Crescent Publishing Co., Aligarh).

Hughes, Thomas Patrick,
DICTIONARY OF ISLAM, (Cosmo Publications, New Delhi, 1982).

Husain, Syed Athar,
THE GLORIOUS CALIPHATE, (Academy of Islamic Research & Publications, Lucknow, 1974).

Iqbal, Sir Muhammad,
THE RECONSTRUCTION OF RELIGIOUS THOUGHT IN ISLAM, (Kitab Publishing House, Delhi, 1974).

Latif Dr. Syed Abdul,
BASES OF ISLAMIC CULTURE, (Idarah-e Adabiyat-e Dilli, Delhi-6, 1977).

Mahmood Dr. Tahir,
MUSLIM PERSONAL LAW, (All India Reporter, Ltd., Nagpur, 1983).

Maududi, Maulana Saiyid Abul A'la,
SHORT HISTORY OF REVIVALIST MOVEMENT IN ISLAM, (Tr. by Al-Ash'ari, Markazi Maktaba Islami, Delhi. 1973).

Nadwi, Maulana Abul Hasan Ali,
SAVIOURS OF ISLAMIC SPIRIT, Vol. I, Tr. by Mohiuddin Ahmad, Academy of Islamic Research & Publications, Lucknow, 1971).

Nadwi, Maulana Abul Hasan Ali,
THE GLORIOUS CALIPHATE, Tr. by Syed Athar Husain, Lucknow).

Nadwi, Maulana Shahabuddin,
ISLAMIC SHARIAH IN INDIA, Bangalore.

Nomani, M.,
AL-FAROOQUE, New Delhi.

Qadri, A. A.,
ISLAMIC JURISPRUDENCE IN THE MODERN WORLD, (N. M. Tripathi, Bombay).

Saduddin,
THE LIFE OF IMAM ABU HANIFA, (Srinagar).

Saiyidain, Dr. K. G.,
ISLAM THE RELIGION OF PEACE, (Jamia Nagar, New Delhi, 1976).

Valiuddin, Dr. Mir,
THE QU'RANIC SUFISM, (Motilal Benarasidass, Delhi).

Watt, W. Montgomery,
ISLAM AND THE INTEGRATION OF SOCIETY, (Routledge & Kegan Paul, London, 1961).

INDEX